GOA TO ME

GOA TO ME

TEOTONIO R. DE SOUZA
Director
Xavier Centre of Historical Research
Alto Porvorim, Goa

Foreword by
PROF. C.R. BOXER

CONCEPT PUBLISHING COMPANY, NEW DELHI-110059

ISBN 81-7022-504-3

First Published 1994

Published and Printed by
Ashok Kumar Mittal
Concept PUblishing Company
A/15-16, Commercial Block, Mohan Garden
NEW DELHI-110059 (India)

Lasertypeset by
Printing Express
H-13, Bali Nagar
NEW DELHI-110015

to

E. A. C.

FOREWORD

DR. TEOTONIO R. DE SOUZA needs no introduction from me or from anyone else, but since he has asked me to provide a brief foreword to this book, I cannot refuse, as I have been for a long time a personal friend and an admirer of his work.

As a loyal son of the soil and an old-timer in the Society of Jesus, he has also been fully aware of the dissident and controversial viewpoints expressed by many writers in many languages. Church and State; Caste and Class; Economy and Society; and many other aspects of religious and socio-economic history have all engaged his attention. Nor does he shrink from controversy, although his standpoints are temperately expressed, and wields no poisoned pen. The old Indo-Portuguese adage that "the nib of a Jesuit's pen is more to be feared than the point of an Arab's sword", is not strictly applicable to his work, which often evinces respect for non-Christian creeds and faiths. The reader will find that these articles range both widely and deeply, with a chronological bracket from the sixteenth century to the present day. They provide profitable and stimulating reading and new insights even for those who are familiar with the topics which are treated.

21 January 1993

C. R. BOXER
Ringshall End, Little Gaddesden,
Berkhamsted, Herts., U.K.

ACKNOWLEDGMENTS

Original versions of the essays collected and revised in this book appeared in different publications as indicated below:

1. *Goa through the Ages: An Economic History*, ed. Teotonio R. de Souza (Goa University Publications Series, No.6), New Delhi, 1989.
2. *Indo-Portuguese History: Sources & Problems,* ed. John Correia–Afonso, Bombay, 1981.
3. *Congresso internacional de história: Missionaçäo portuguesa e encontro de culturas: Actas*, Vol. IV, Braga, 1993.
4. *Goa: Cultural Trends*, ed. P.P. Shirodkar, Panjim, Goa, 1988.
5. *Studies in the Foreign Relations of India:* From the earliest times to 1947, ed. P.M. Joshi and M. A. Nayeem, Hyderabad, 1975.
6. *II Seminário internacional de história indo-portuguesa: Actas,* ed. Luis de Albuquerque e Inácio Guerreiro, Lisboa, 1985.
7. *Indo-Portuguese History: Old Issues, New Questions*, ed. Teotonio R. de Souza, New Delhi, 1985.
8. *VI Seminário internacional de história indo-portuguesa: Actas,* ed. Artur Teodoro de Matos e L.F. e Reis Thomaz, Macau, 1993.
9. *Goa Today,* Panjim, Goa, March 1987.
10. *Goa Today,* Panjim, Goa, December 1986.

My old friend Prof. C. R. Boxer has a unique gift of encouraging young scholars. I was privileged to be one of those beneficiaries of his patronage. This has continued ever since his first rave review of my *Medieval Goa* in 1979. His Foreword to this little book is the latest testimony of his unflagging virtue.

Mario Miranda has his own rightful place in Goa's cultural heritage. His cover design and other sketches have added the characteristic touch of *Goa of Mario* to *Goa to me.* I am deeply grateful to him for this and for his appreciation of my work at all times.

My grateful thanks are due to my colleague and friend Rev. Dr. Charles Borges, S.J. who went carefully through the text wordprocessed by my office secretary and patient assistant Ms. Ernesta Bhobe.

TEOTONIO R. DE SOUZA

CONTENTS

INTRODUCTION

It is not by mere accident that the title of this book bears a resemblance to Emily Hahn's *China to me* (N.Y., 1944). I had heard of the book and the ripples it made when it appeared. I have often been a guest of the author at her home in U.K., whenever I dropped in to greet my old friend and mentor Prof. Charles Boxer and to update my knowledge about the latest in the Portuguese expansion history. When Prof. Boxer sent me the text of the **Foreword**, I was not decided about the title. I was thinking about it, when another good friend Bob Newman, an American anthropologist and a friend of India of the Peace Corps times, dropped in on his usual surprise visits and brought me a gift, which he thought I would surely appreciate. It was Emily Hahn's *China to me*. It decided for me what I should call my book of collected essays, but there would be no 60 chapters, neither would it run into 424 pages, nor would it be a new book.

Goa to me brings together ten dispersed essays out of all that I published during the past two decades. The readers looking for the kind of stuff that precedes and follows the Battle of Shouson Hill in Emily Hahn's partial autobiography may feel left somewhat in the cold. To save them from total disappointment I thought of providing a unifying backdrop for the contents, for my involvement in historical research, for my concerns underlying the choice of the themes, and for my style of formulation of the essays in the form of an autobiographical introduction. It is hoped that this feature will make it more of a lived history, rather than an abstract description of historical scenarios. My autobiographical disclosures may lack the spice of the challenging mix of the flippant and heroic romance of *China to me*, but it may not be devoid of some weak parallels. If Emily Hahn's Charles "walked, and talked and drank like an Army officer", while he was decidedly not "a straight military type", the same has been said or kept prudently unsaid by many who have known the author of the present book. They may wonder how he has retained his affiliation to the Society of Jesus this long, crossing a quarter century, and handling responsible jobs as a *solemnly professed* member of the Order. That is one of the secrets of the success of the

Order which knows to recognise the frailty as well as the heroic ingredients of the human nature. Perhaps I was able to display some heroism and considerable achievement in spite of my many frailties, all because of this magnanimous approach of the Order.

However, while the Order has to go on exercising its charism, an individual member may need to respond to the calls of his conscience elsewhere. Perseverance in vocation is stressed in the culture of the Orders as an important grace, because it is necessary for the survival of the Orders. But it can also become for some of its members a virtuous cover for security of undisturbed life and professional success, or for shunning the embarrassment of being accused of inconsistency of character, if not something worse. I hold in high esteem some of the Jesuits known to me and who had the courage of conviction to opt out. Such decisions have helped these individuals to accept sincerely the need for change with changed circumstances in their lives, but they have also helped often to purify those who opted to continue their commitment in the Order.

The essays selected for this book may not have found and may still not win the approval of some who wish to see Goa differently. But this is *Goa to me*. I hope that my autobiographical disclosures, even though partial, will enable those whose sentiments may have been hurt by my writings and research activities over the past many years to adopt a more forgiving or sympathetic attitude. But this is no plea to seek indulgence for my follies, both past and those to come. I confess that I do not consider myself a superhuman "Paulist" of 16th century Goan fame, and much less an angel incarnate. However, I could claim in all sincerity that I have relentlessly sought to understand the bends and twists of life, both personal and of the community at various levels, and sought to make a positive contribution to it. Obviously, my own life has been the point of departure for these efforts, and as such, it has coloured and shaped the process. There has been much in it, as one would say, to write home about, but it has not been without a share of tragedy (in the original Greek sense of the term). No borrowed wisdom seems to suffice to discern how far one is letting things happen to oneself, rather than directing the course of events that make one's life. That is where the tragedy and the implied *nemesis* come in. In spite of having lived for over quarter of a century in the Society of Jesus with its dominant western and rational culture, the oriental in me cannot help sharing with oriental Jesus the tendency to believe in the hour that has come or has not come.

I shall try to be less abstract: My *Goa to me* began unfolding itself in a Goan village in the late forties. It was a village with the unsavoury privilege of being qualified for a kind of wisdom that did not fit in the accepted categories of normality. But because of that the inhabitants of

Moirá have gained a privileged niche in the local folklore. No one would be surprised if they heard of a Moidekar manuring the foundations of his Church to see it grow, or to see him opening another hole at the bottom of a canoe to let out the water seeping in, and so on and so forth. Someone, who pretends to be too wise and demanding, is also condemned by the traditional Goan folk wisdom to belong to the company of the wise fools of Moirá. This is quite picturesquely expressed in the local proverb — *Ragar fugar zali, xekim Moiddea kazar zali* — conveying the fate of a girl who tried to be extra choosy, and ended up marrying a Moidekar! The only redeeming feature about the village inhabitants was that they produced a very special and much wanted variety of bananas! However, a sympathetic observer wishing to go beyond the stereotypes could discover a village of hard-working people, and with a marked ability to occupy respectable public positions while pursuing routine agricultural and other activities that required a manner of dress and attire that jarred sharply with the white collar mentality of the middle classes. To a Moidekar it was a routine change from his *kashty* (loin cloth) to the office suit and *vice versa*.

My grandfather, *ganvkar* of the fifth *vangad* of the village, was at least a 16th generation Catholic descendant of Shantappa Kamat, who became Diogo de Souza after his conversion to Christianity early in the seventeenth century. Joaquim Rosário de Souza, who had no formal education, neither did he see the need of any for his children, was quite conversant with Portuguese administrative jargon. No interested village *ganvkar* felt confident to proceed with the periodic auctioning of the paddy fields if "Lam Jaku" (Tall Joaquim) or "Jaku Tiu" (Uncle Joaquim), as my grandfather was respectfully or affectionately called, was not available to check the correctness of the field measurements. It might take a modern expert a bit longer today to calculate as fast as he did without any aid of paper and pen or calculators. Thirty-five years after the death of the octogenarian, his more or less illustrious descendants are still better known in the village as children or grandchildren of *Lam Jaku*! He never drank liquor in excess, but he had the choicest vocabulary of bad words in Konkani and Konkanised Portuguese (though never in public) against those who belonged to the "pants-wearing" class, or *Calção-kar* as he termed it! He wore them also, along with a *Nehru*-cut black *judi*. But that was because the Portuguese law required it for those entering the capital or a provincial town. *Lam Jaku* would get rid of these sartorial requisites as soon as he had finished his job in the town and crossed the town limits to return home. It was from

him that I learned my first lessons of Goan history. Besides, as a child till five or six years of age, I would only sleep in the lap of my grandma. Her folk tales were a great attraction. But I do not remember having heard a complete story ever! After the exhaustion of day's pranks it was too difficult to keep awake that long.

My grandfather had *Rosário* as his second name, and my grandma was Maria *Rosária* Pinto. From them both, who were also my godparents, I inherited my second name, but more importantly they had sown in me a love for my culture. Close to the ground and the fields, my grandmother assisted me in identifying and naming in my mother-tongue at least nine different types of ants! It may sound ridiculous, but I have never ceased giving the Goan ants a special place in my understanding of Goan culture. All the more so, because I have not been able as yet to find so many entomological designations for those ants in Portuguese language or in English. An *umlo, a domlo, a katt-mui, a ganed'di mui, a danvteri mui, a chabkuri mui, valloi* and *pott-valloi*, and the nests of *un'na* were an integral part of my *Goa to me*, even though they troubled me often as a child with down to earth occupations.

My father was the third child and the second son of *Lam Jaku*, who had seven children as did his parents. Luis Caetano was the only son who frequented the parish school on his own initiative, and he learned to read and write with books donated by his friendly companions. But with no further encouragement at home he had to discontinue his studies in order to join the other siblings in the fields. The joint efforts of the family earned them no more than Rs. 14 per week during the best of times. After reserving about Rs. 300 for paying the annual land revenue to the State, they had little left to think of anything beyond subsistence. It was through an elderly neighbour working in Hyderabad that my father found his way to the city of Nizam as a hotel boy and started on a monthly salary of Rs. 15. After six years in Hyderabad he shifted to Bombay hotels obtaining a pay rise of Rs. 70. With his earnings he helped his parents to pay at least half of the annual dues to the State, as well as to meet other extraordinary home expenses and to pay the dowries to marry his three younger sisters. As a result he had no savings when he decided in 1942 to marry a Goan girl he had never met before. But this young bride from the island village of Malar and with many educated people and high clergy in her family and among her relatives brought a new sense of discipline and literacy awareness into the family of her in-laws. To her relatively enlightened outlook, the life with the in-laws was a torture, and more so when she had to bring up her two sons without the assistance of the husband, who had succeeded in migrating to Kuwait in 1949 in search of better prospects. My elder brother Calisto was five then, and myself a toddler of two. Our only sister Milagrina (Christie) would arrive five years later when the life conditions had brightened a little with some shine of the Kuwaiti dinars. But soon would come the "economic blockade" imposed by Indian authorities and the tax imposed by the Portuguese authorities on the remittances of the emigrants.

We were doubly hit and some other circumstances would make it harder at times. I remember one such instance: My mother never let us know the problems of the adults, and would always spare a Rupee each to me and to my brother on the village feast day to purchase whatever we wished in the fair. In 1955 her purse was picked in the town market on the eve of the village feast. She had nothing left to give us, and I observed her sobbing and praying before the family oratory. Next morning she had conjured two rupees for her sons. Obviously she had borrowed them from a neighbour. My brother spent his rupee in the fair as usual, but I decided to return my one rupee to my mother giving a silly reason for my action. I still remember her grateful eyes, but she said nothing. It was only some years ago before she died recently (1991) that I narrated that incident to her only to realise that she had never forgotten my act of good sense at that early age.

If I have gone into narrating the above details, it is chiefly to introduce the life conditions that prevailed in a Goan village. Mine was not an isolated lot. It was rather a representative picture of the great majority of the village people. It was truly the "idiocy of the rural life", to borrow an expression from Karl Marx. One could count on one's finger-tips the families in the village doing well for themselves. These were closely associated with the Portuguese administration, and some of them had even acquired a colour change. The other reason for narrating some very personal experiences is to disclose one crucial factor that shaped my future for me: A rather premature ability to observe my surroundings and to draw my conclusions. It has been a boon and a bane of my life. I could sense that something was terribly amiss with the village life. I could see that my mother could make some headway in directing our family affairs only to the extent she sought and obtained help and patronage of some of the rich families of the village. I had as a school mate a son of one of these families while doing my Portuguese primary studies. His parents patronised us the most, but it should go to their credit that they never made us feel humiliated for that. But since my colleague came from a Portuguese speaking family, I could hardly compete with him in studying a language that was entirely alien to my home culture, despite the "specialised" vocabulary of my grandfather. But even so I did fairly and comparably well. This acted as a catalyst in my decision to join the seminary after completing the primary studies at the age of 10. Why seminary ? My school mate was going there, and hence my continued desire to gain at least some equality with him. I also believed very innocently then that the priests in the seminary would do more justice to me. There was another important reason and that is intimately bound up with my *Goa to me*: The only other educational alternatives after primary studies, were the private English high school in the village and the Portuguese Lyceum in the capital city of Panjim. The first alternative was viable and my brother opted for it. But I was aware of the additional economic burden on my parents had I too done the same. The second alternative was ruled out for a village boy of my means. If one knows the medieval means of public transport in Goa of those days, even with some money one was discouraged from frequenting Panjim every day; and the privilege of finding residential quarters in the capital was not for the lesser mortals. Hence, the seminary was the only hope for the ambitious of the low middle class. The studies were subsidised with freeships. Many flocked to the seminary from all corners of Goa, and many abandoned it with equal hurry or at different stages. But my personal background advised a calculated perseverance. I was only ten years old when I joined, and I feared to return to the rural idiocy. Hence I persevered, completed the minor seminary studies, and donned the soutane to enter the major seminary. By then the liberation of Goa had taken place, and it also had a deep impact on my personal surroundings and life. I could see the heretofore ruling families of our village visibly collapsing into social insignificance. A new sense of self dignity was felt by the rural folk and they could see this translated in the new political scenario that began to unfold itself. Educational facilities became more widely available, and there was a sudden spurt of development as never seen before. I could see the impact of this change also reflected in the attitude of the priests in the seminary. Some of them too saw no future for their pretensions and for providing preferential treatment to some students coming from certain prominent families, specially those with influential *tio-padres* (uncle priests). In this process I experienced suddenly a greater appreciation of my intellectual capabilities, and from a mediocre scorer I had become *urso do curso* (luminary of the class) as my late and distinguished teacher of Portuguese literature, Rev. Filinto Cristo Dias, expressed in public once. There had to be a break of the entire system to bring about such a change of attitudes and opportunities. And I was confirmed in my assessment of the situation even as a child. But that did not make me less of a victim of that system. Even after the system had vanished, and fresh wind was blowing, the scars would remain and also some internal wounds to be healed.

Poor diet, though rich in carbohydrates (rice in the morning, rice in the evening, rice at every meal and also in between meals), was greatly responsible for the weak body formation and little resistance to diseases. Problems connected with hygiene were part of the idiocy of rural life. Medical facilities were primitive, and my brother and myself had to be taken to Bombay via Majali and Karwar to undergo operations for tonsilitis. Actually, it was only recommended for my brother, but to save a possible repetition of costs with another trip, my tonsils were taken away as well. That was in 1959. It is very likely that the nature took its revenge, and a couple of years later I was struck by *streptococci.* Without immediate diagnosis and treatment for the rheumatic fever in the seminary boarding, I was left somewhat handicapped for life. The heart murmur had set in, and its one visible effect was my inability to keep up with my mad interest in playing football. Till then my life in the seminary had been great fun: No time or interest for Latin or other studies, but I had all the time for planning football tournaments. By four o'clock in the afternoon I would start enlisting team mates and pumping football! I had no sympathy for those colleagues who showed no interest in joining my team or at least the opponent team. There was always a sizable number of such colleagues who preferred to do garden work or just go for walks. But the damage to my mitral heart valve turned the tables on me: I joined the company of the evening walkers. However,

one positive result of it all was that it dawned on me that I would have to study better to compensate. My performance improved dramatically from then onwards. The changed socio-political scenario described earlier had enhanced the change within me.

I have mentioned two factors that brought about my enlightenment. I cannot ignore yet another that lay dormant and to which I had till then refused to pay heed: It was my mother. I have already referred to her background and her concerns. She was also a very pious lady, who was determined to bring up her children in traditional religious ways. Praying the rosary was a daily evening ritual before we could get our meal. The monotonous ritual usually put me to sleep, and it was my mother's problem afterwards to wake me up sufficiently to find my mouth to eat. But even before the recitation of the rosary, we had yet another item on the daily routine. Our outdoor games had to end at the ringing of the Church bell for *Angelus* around sunset, and then my mother would sit with me and my brother to make us repeat some of the formulas of the catechism. This too we did with great reluctance. And at the end of that session she would admonish us about various current issues at home or about our behaviour outdoors. One refrain was never absent: "Unless you study, you will be fit only to drive bullock cart"! I never liked to hear that compliment, and I had even developed the habit of irritating her by blocking my ears with my fingers. But she persisted with the routine despite her many other occupations till I joined the seminary. As a result of my resistance her admonitions sank deeper into me, and they remained in my subconscious till the ground was ripe for them to show positive result. What had convinced me more than her instructions were the sincerity of her concern for her children, and the burden and worries she endured bravely without our father to assist her physically during all those difficult years. As a good "third world mother" she died prematurely of sheer exhaustion. Aided by these memories, my respect for her never allowed me to add to her sufferings while she lived, even when I knew that I had to take certain life decisions which I considered overdue. Even a suggestion of it once threw her into fits: She had raised the public image of the family with so much care and pains. How could I let her down? That is what her reaction implied. My father would always stand by her, even when she was wrong. But left to himself, he let us do what we deemed right. He is no less pious and traditional, but his wider exposure to the world beyond Goa made him more liberal and less hypertense. He has crossed 80 and is blessed to continue possessing the earth!

Rachol seminary has a history of its own, and I became part of it when I lived and studied philosophy there for three years. I went there because I did not have sufficient courage to go anywhere else. My Portuguese studies of the seminary were not going to be of much acceptance in the new changed academic scenario of Goa after liberation. I would have to start English studies afresh. My best bet was to continue and keep looking out for a promising break. As dictated by my enlightenment I performed very well in my studies, but my inner tensions and worry about the future took much of the cheer out of my life. The rheumatic heart grew more rheumatic under such depression. I experienced frequent fits of giddiness. I alone knew what was causing them. I had also assessed the limited avenues for personal growth as a diocesan priest in Goa. I was desperately looking for an escape route.

Every seminary has a "spiritual director", and Rachol seminary had a tradition of having a resident Jesuit to do that job. Originally it was a Jesuit college and from there the Jesuits fanned out to the whole of Salcete to implant Christianity. Some of them paid a heavy price for it, but not without extracting a heavy price from many natives as well. The contents of this book will go into the merits of this contentious issue. The suppression of the Society of Jesus by Marquis of Pombal was not entirely delinked from it, and my colleague Dr. Charles Borges has discussed it at length in his doctoral dissertation on the "Economics of Goa Jesuits before Suppression, 1542-1759". But I was quite ignorant then of all the implications of the Jesuit zeal in Goan history or of European expansion in general. While in Rachol seminary I came to know two Jesuits and both impressed me by their zeal and competence. One of them was a bearded care-taker of the relics of St. Francis Xavier. He preached a retreat to the seminarians. But another Jesuit was resident as spiritual father and impressed me by his ability to master Konkani language and to contribute with words and music to the renewal of the Church liturgy in the wake of the second Vatican Council. I confided to him the reasons for my dissatisfaction, and he promptly saw in me a likely candidate for his Order. Besides, the Jesuits of Goa were just then planning to inaugurate a new Novitiate house in Belgaum. It suited my needs. I would have the desired break, and I could hope to switch on to formation in English and perhaps would make it to a college degree. My brother had by then completed his degree in Science at St. Xavier's College in Bombay, and I did not want to be left behind only with the traditional Goan clerical formation.

I had come to the end of my studies of philosophy at Rachol. I went to inform the Rector that I was planning to discontinue my stay in the seminary to join the Jesuits. I did not get an impression that he would lose his sleep because of it, but he was polite enough to tell me that the doors would remain open if I decided to change my mind. There was no question of my changing my mind. It was not an opportunity to be missed and quick action followed. The seminarians were attending the consecration of the new Vicar Apostolic of Goa, Mgr. F.X. Rebelo, at the See Cathedral in Old Goa, and the Jesuit Provincial Superior would be present. It was arranged for me to meet him there. I had found out that he descended partly from my village. This little detail made me feel more at ease. My admission was decided on the spot. The required formalities followed, and in June of 1967 I was leaving my family with my small trunk and a violin to join the Jesuit Novitiate in Desur near Belgaum. It was the end of one big chapter in my life. I felt the loss of some of my dear colleagues with whom I had shared my life for over a decade. Bui I realised over time that real friends are never lost. And after 25 years even my link with Rachol seminary was revived when I was asked by the Archbishop-Patriarch to assist in the setting up of a Museum of Christian Art in the premises of the seminary. It gave me an opportunity in 1991 to prepare the first ever illustrated inventory of most of the art objects in the diocese. This inventory set the rest of the project in motion and I look forward to its success and steady growth. I see it as yet another positive consequence of the bends and twists in my life.

I may have given an impression that my every move was a calculated move and purely utilitarian. It was never exactly so. Noble ideals, including even dreams of dying a martyr, had not been absent at some stages of my training in the two seminaries. But I began to understand slowly that these were not truly expressions of a healthy sublimation, neither my drive to achieve name and fame was a way of seeking a healthy compensation. There was a yawning gap left in the emotional growth by a forced long jump from childhood into adulthood, or from the womb to the tomb, to quote a counsellor friend who described this problem of child vocations to celibate priesthood. I can still recall the weekly exhortations of the spiritual father in the minor seminary harping on the need to control immoral thoughts, and to avoid looking at provocative nude or seminude pictures and the like. Such exhortations were all the more intense on the eve of mid-term and summer vacations. I do not recall having had any anxiety about sex before I joined the seminary. The seminary formation succeeded in implanting and nurturing obsessions that left me struggling during years and years that followed to rectify the damage done and to regain a positive approach to sexuality and to relationship with women. Only my happy experiences of childhood contributed to minimise the damage. Fortunately the seminaries today are more aware of these problems and recruit persons who have grown through normal adolescence in normal life situations. If some seminaries still do not do this, they are likely to perpetuate the evils of celibacy, instead of promoting it as the noblest expression of commitment to serve others beyond one's choice.

I could breathe more freely in every possible way in the new surroundings and style of life in the Jesuit Novitiate. The Novitiate programme provided the calm that my nerves badly required. Most of my companions were comparatively younger than me in age, in academic formation, as well as in experiences of religious training. Hence, I was not required to go through the usual stages of the Jesuit training, such as Juniorate or Regency. I was asked to enroll myself in the Pontifical Athenaeum in Poona soon after the first two years of Novitiate to revise my studies of philosophy and to obtain a Licentiate degree in one year. It was a tall order for someone whose seminary training in philosophical studies was largely restricted to memorising definitions in Latin. Under the cover of badly understood Latin there was only a heap of philosophical ignorance and pretensions. I was qualified with *accessit* in these! At the Athenaeum it was different. I could appreciate the value of philosophical training, and I performed too well even for my own expectations. Even before I knew it, the Dean of the Faculty had approached my Provincial Superior to seek his permission to spare me for the teaching staff. Though such an invitation would be eagerly accepted by many, it held no attraction for me.

I had set my heart on graduating myself in History at the University. I needed to have the training that would qualify me to find satisfactory answers to what I had grown to understand as historical questions that had affected my life in *Goa to me*. I conveyed to the Superiors my disinterest in teaching philosophy, and I was granted permission to enroll for M.A. in History at the University of Poona on condition that I would at least consider teaching Church History. I had learned to cross a bridge when I came to it. So I agreed to consider the suggestion. The University of Poona was very considerate in those days to grant equivalence to the Licentiate degree of the Athenaeum, and I was allowed to join. It was for me the beginning of the realisation of a dream, specially against the background of no educational training in English. In the seminary we were taught English as a second language, and it was only in the Jesuit Novitiate that I had mastered the written and spoken English.

I concluded yet another phase of studies with flying colours, scoring the highest marks that year in the Faculty of Arts and being eligible for some prizes of the University as well as a Junior Research Fellowship of the University Grants Commission if I wished to start research leading to Ph.D. The Department of History regarded that as a credit also to itself, and the Head of the Department showed keen interest in my future studies. One major block was to obtain a clearence of my Superiors. It was not a common practice in those days to allow a Jesuit at this stage to pursue doctoral studies. However, the insistence from the University professor who offered to guide my research finally prevailed, but only after he had personally discussed the matter with my Superiors. This intervention of Prof. A. R. Kulkarni set me quite decisively on the road to my achievements in my career as a historian. He has ever since remained my *guru*, and accompanied me with a paternal concern.

I had shifted my base to Goa in 1972 to utilise the documentation available in the Goa State Archives and other public libraries. I had at last the opportunity to clarify for myself the historical legacy that had affected and shaped my life in so many ways. The first essay selected for inclusion in this book is also the longest one. It had to be so, because it represents the hard core of my research contribution to Goa's history. It was a gratifying experience to see that my *Medieval Goa* (1979) was received internationally with very positive reviews. The first English edition is sold out and the book is still in demand and its Portuguese version is due to be out. What happened much before that in a quiet way was more important. That was in 1973, while I was at a Jesuit High School residence in Goa. A new Provincial Superior, Fr. Romuald de Souza, a Columbia trained clinical psychologist, whom I had never met before came to discuss my progress and life plans. He had done his home-work and knew about my reluctance to be on the teaching staff of the Pontifical Athenaeum. To my great surprise he considered it as a very hopeful sign! He explained to me his plans to raise the level of the Jesuit educational involvement in Goa. If I would cooperate, he would create facilities for an historical research institute in Goa. I could not think of anything better. It just fitted into my scheme of things. The seed of the Xavier Centre of Historical Research was thus sown, and the germination process started.

I was allowed to pay my first visit to European archives at the end of that same year. It turned out to be a more memorable visit because it coincided with the end of the Salazar era in Portugal on 25th of April 1974. It augured well for my historical concerns. It led to improvement of relations between Portugal and India, and I could more easily return to Portugal in 1977 to seek the backing of the Calouste Gulbenkian Foundation for our plans in Goa. The planning for the Institute continued at various levels, and I was personally involved at every stage of it.

It was during this process that I came under strong influence of Fr. Romuald de Souza, and I grew in the understanding of Jesuit ways of planning and executing. The third person whose influence was greatly beneficial in my formation was Fr. John Correia-Afonso, a Jesuit with vast experience of administration in the Society of Jesus, as one time Provincial Superior of Bombay Jesuits, Principal of St. Xavier's College (Bombay) more than once, and as Counsellor and Secretary to the General of the Society of Jesus in Rome. It was in his capacity as Director of the Heras Institute of Indian History and Culture (Bombay) that I had to deal with him and seek his collaboration with our plans. We had decided that he should be officially the first Director of the new Institute in Goa, while I would be an Associate Director attending to the ordinary running of the Institute in Goa. This arrangement was necessary because I had still to complete the required priestly formation in theology in Poona and get myself ordained.

While the professional planning was progressing marvellously well, my personal life was running on a different track, and the two never synchronised well despite apparent harmony. I had no choice but to silence the inner crying of my conscience in order to sustain the progress on professional front. This did not prevent me from performing very well once again at the academic level in theological formation. However, I was not convinced or enamoured of the contents of most of the Church dogmas, with the exception of the incarnation and resurrection of Jesus, and some other beliefs. Even in these cases my understanding certainly differed from the official explanations. I wonder if this is a proper place to discuss the mystery of Holy Trinity, but considering my understanding of it, any place should be good for it. It seems to convey one central need of human society, namely the need to accept hierarchy of functions and yet function as a unified whole with mutual concern and love. It makes great sense to me, but I am not sure if anything I have read in treatises of theology or heard in many eloquent sermons has ever helped me to appreciate the message of this central mystery. I never saw the usefulness of raising any serious questions on these issues, knowing well the fundamentalist backlash that could affect my prospects at this stage. On this and many other scores things do not seem to have changed greatly since the days of Jesus. In spite of my reluctance to pronounce on these matters I could not resist being drawn into the acitivities of the Ecumenical Association of the Third World Theologians, but more as a historian than as a theologian. This should suffice to clarify my stands in some of the essays in this book, as well as in several others that figure in my list of writings appended to it.

The Xavier Centre of Historical Research came officially into existence in 1977, but it ceased to be only on the paper in November 1979. It marked the realisation of my life dream. It moved from strength to strength and by 1986 the Goa University could not ignore its merits. It was granted affiliation and could enroll scholars for doctoral research under my orientation. Two of these early candidates have already qualified themselves. More achievements can be read in the published annual reports of the Institute and its research publications are widely in circulation. Despite strong initial resistance from various lay persons that sought to block the project at official and unofficial levels, the Institute continued its march of progress, and in the course of time many older opponents became its best supporters. I have to confess that a change of my own personal attitudes was required to bring about such an improvement in relations. Also many historical prejudices against the Jesuits in Goa had to be allayed. This should also shed light on what may be considered by my own Jesuit colleagues and traditional Christian well-wishers of the Institute as an unwarranted and over-critical assessment of the Church history or Jesuit history. However, in adopting such stands for the sake of strategy I have at no stage chosen to sacrifice historical truth, or preferred one bias for another.

I do, however, owe an open apology to our former Portuguese colonizers. My early writings were too harsh on them and I tended to attribute to them more evils than those for which they may have been responsible. My feelings of hostility directed against the present-day descendants of the colonizers were certainly misplaced. However, I wish that they will understand it as my over-reaction to my own past and not entirely to theirs. In the process of two decades of research and closer personal contacts with the Portuguese helped me to realise that there were our well-wishers among them, while many enemies of our people came also from within. This continues to be the reality till date. Some of my writings, including a couple of essays in this book, illustrate this point. Positively, we owe it to the Portuguese to have exposed us to the wider world much earlier than many other people of our country and subcontinent. This does not apply only to the Christians of Goa, though these are at times mistakenly and maliciously regarded by some communally-biased political interests as the chief beneficiaries and even collaborators of the former colonial masters. Many of my writings, starting with *Medieval Goa* have thoroughly proved the contrary had often been true.

I would be failing in my duty if I did not record here my gratitude to many friends who have effectively backed and even suffered in many ways to enable me to make the positive contribution I could make to my people and to the world of knowledge at large. I can mention among these Fr. Übelmesser, S.J. (Germany) and Fr. Kilian Hönle and friends from Süssen (Germany), as well as Rev. Dr. Bacelar e Oliveira, S.J. and Dr. José Blanco (Portugal). Closer at home some have already been mentioned earlier in these pages. I still need to mention a former provincial superior, Fr. Leslie Almeida, S.J. who stood by me most patiently when I had already come to a road block in life ten years ago. Whether the time was gained or lost is more for the others to judge, but I have seen its many benefits. Fr. Charles Borges, S.J. has been a supportive colleague at work and a friend since 1981 through many difficult times and situations. Fr. Cajetan Coelho, S.J. and Fr. Délio Mendonça, S.J. are two junior colleagues whose serious involvement in historical research has relieved greatly my worries about the future of the Institute. I cherish more their most sypathetic sharing of my problems and willingness to help out within their possibilities. There have been a few other persons who sustained me emotionally and otherwise at various stages of my life. I know that they do not wish to be named here, but I can never forget their concern and their contribution to my personal growth. To one of them this book is dedicated, as an acknowledgment of my past failures and shortcomings, and a promise to rectify them. It is for this very reason that *Goa to me* has a special significance at this juncture.

I wish to present this book as my homage to Goa and to the new Goa Province of the Society of Jesus, both of which I have loved and served with all my heart and mind, and to the point of forgetting my soul, even if this should appear questionable to some in certain contexts. But I should leave it to history to clarify. Despite its shortcomings, it is a better judge of our actions and intentions, achievements and failures. I do believe in historical objectivity. It is a sum total of the subjective reconstructions of individual historians. I shall leave the readers with *Goa to me*, my insider's viewpoints and contribution to an eventual objective history of my land and my people. If one needs to know the historian for understanding what he writes, I hope I have come to the assistance of the reader in this respect. Village communities and their *Lam Jaku*, western missionaries with the State backing and their white colonial superiority *vis-à-vis* the *milagristas* of Fr. Joseph Vaz and their native approach, the Panjim-based Mhamai *sarkar vis-à-vis* Calcutta-Macau-Bombay based opium dealer Rogerio de Faria who yearned for his native *pátria*, the Ranes of Goan folklore, and a Church that was reduced to a willing or helpless handmaid of the colonial masters, are an assorted presentation for understanding the complex texture of the history and culture of Goa as it has evolved till our own days.

1

GOAN VILLAGE: Economy and Life

Goa's rural economy cannot be treated as purely agrarian, and it can be best understood only against the background of its littoral nature at the cross-roads of coastal trade lines. The term *Shashti* (Salcete taluka) may have been understood by most scholars in terms parallel to Bardesh or Tiswadi or Sattari, pointing to the number of land settlements, but it could also have something to do with the Ocean (*Shastha*) that fed its early settlers and continued to play a significant role in its economy. The Kadamba Shastadevas ruling from Chandrapur took their titles to signify their control over the Ocean, and not any number of land divisions. This geographical factor has determined substantially Goa's historical economic-cultural development. Though it was linked to the hinterland, with the arrival of the Portuguese and its strategic constraints, these links were kept to the minimum and Goa became more of a colonial enclave with more extensive connections with the outside. These factors have been taken into consideration in this brief essay on the Goan rural economy and life. This chapter will, therefore, go beyond agrarian economy and cover such aspects as development of crafts and the hinterland trade. The Goan village communities were far from being isolated and self-sufficient economic units.

Early Cultural Developments

Goa was part and parcel of the Indian subcontinent in its historical evolution. The interplay of the cultures brought to Goa across the Sahayadri range of hills in the east and the Ocean in the west, has left an indelible impression on various aspects of cultural development of Goa through the passage of time. The antiquities and remains throwing light on the cultural development of Goa since pre-historic times such as stone implements and pottery, temples ruins, pieces of sculptures, lithic and copper-plate records of pious grants by different rulers are found scattered all over the territory.[1]

The archaeological evidence in the form of polished stone-axe, suggesting the first settlement of the land by the Neolithic man, has been traced back to 2000 B.C., though it is suggested that Kols, Kharvis and Mundaris may have been the first settlers of Goa, living on fishing, hunting and primitive form of agriculture since c. 3500 B.C. The Neolithic culture was succeeded by the iron age (c. 1200 B.C.) which was known during the period of *Mahabharata.* This is described in the *pauranic* tradition of Parashurama, the sixth incarnation of god Vishnu. He is said to have reclaimed the Konkan strip of land from the sea, including Govarashtra, one of its seven divisions. The myth implies the arrival of *parashu* or axe that could help the clearance of the dense forests of the Konkan and permit a more extensive and permanent settlement.[2] This legend of Parashurama occurs all along the west coast and is related to the route and pattern of colonisation from Punjab to Kerala along the sea-shore. It appears that Gujarati navigators played an important role in this process, and hence their sailing tradition goes far beyond the advent of Islam. The sea-expeditions of the Bhargavas of Gujarat, armed with axes and bows must have left a deep impression on the primitive tribals who were using crude stone and wood implements. The impression was exploited by successive Aryan settlers and the feudalisation by force was completed with cultural paraphernalia of Brahminism and the caste system.[3].

During the Mauryan period and strong trade contacts with the Middle East and Alexandrian empire the influence of Jainism and Buddhism became predominant in Goa. This influence can be still found in the place names and in the language. Even though some of the rock caves found in Goa are considered as Brahmanical and dated as belonging to seventh to ninth centuries, it is more likely that they were Buddhist. Buddhism had the patronage of the Bhoja rulers just as Jainism had the patronage of the Kadambas. The caves at Lamganv (in Divcholi taluka), as the name of the place itself suggests, were definitely of Buddhist origin. Some of these caves were later occupied by the Shaivites who installed *lingas* and *nandis* in them when the Kadambas opted for Shaivism around c. 12th A.D.[4] Even the Konkani word *buyer* for cave suggests its derivation from *vihara*[5].

As suggested by the early inscriptional evidence, Goa was an important trade centre since very early times. And considering the fact of Buddhist influence, one can also think of the presence of rich magnates of the *mahasala* type mentioned in the Pali literature. They constituted the ruling class of the contemporary society, running plantations and other estates, as suggested by the insights of D.D. Kosambi. [6] The existence of Marcela (*Mashel* in Ponda taluka), may be clarified by this reading. The state of the socio-economic-political organization in Goa during the times for which we have some inscriptional evidence seems to be of a type that shared attributes of both kinds of feudalism mentioned by Kosambi, namely feudalism from above and feudalism from below.[7] As seen in other chapters, Goa was ruled by powerful and less powerful feudatories at different times, but there had developed also a class of land-owners within the multiplicity of villages organized into *desas*, *mahals* or *tanadarias*. There is no indication that rents were collected directly by royal officials as was the case in feudalism from above. There was a local oligarchy of super-*ganvkars* or *desais* and *sardesais* who could retain enough surplus in their hands to assure the trader of steady customers and supplies. The earliest list of customs duties dates from the eleventh century. A copper-plate of Jayakeshi I lists the various lands in sea-contact with *Gopakapur*. This does not by itself give us much information about the nature of hinterland trade and commerce, but it speaks of the works of charity for the poor and revenues set aside to look after them. It is a pointer to urbanization and helpless rural folks coming to seek fortune in the city and finding themselves stranded. [8] The port-town like Goa could not survive without a continuous supply of victuals and other necessities from the neighbouring and more distant hinterland. The Portuguese conqueror of Goa, Afonso de Albuquerque, was well aware of the strategic location of Goa on the coast, but he also mentioned in his report to his king that abundant and easy supplies were locally available to maintain Goa after conquest.[9] And such supplies came from the villages of Tisvadi, Bardez, Salcete, and from what came to be part of Goa as New Conquests in the mid eighteenth century, as well as from the Balghat (Deccan). They came by land routes as well as through riverine waterways. With the decline of the Portuguese sea-trade fortunes the public income depended more on the *rendas* based on the mainland resources. [10]

Inland Trade and Rural Goa

As a very traditional and rudimentary form of inland trade that was common all over the country, Goan villages also had their weekly markets and seasonal fairs that enabled the villagers to dispose of their surplus produce, whether of agriculture or domestic crafts, and to procure in exchange other provisions that they needed.[11] The Portuguese administration had very early during the period of conquest exempted the natives from any tax on the food provisions bought and sold by them within the Portuguese jurisdiction of Goa, but we do come across attempts at different times to bring such transactions under taxation inviting protests of the native population.[12]

In 1526 the State Revenue Superintendent Afonso Mexia ordered a collation of customary practices relating to various past forms of State taxation and revenue administration in the villages as well as in the city suburbs. That is how we have the so-called *Foral* or Charter of Afonso Mexia, and lists of various tariff rates put into effect at the various check-posts (*passos*) leading into the city of Goa, such as Panjim, Mandovi, Daugim, Agasaym, Benasteri, and Narve. These documents published in part by Cunha Rivara in Vol. V of his *Archivo Portuguez-Oriental* give a fairly good idea of the nature of provisions that were brought to the city by the Muslims, native Christians and the Hindus (*"mouros, canarins e gentios da terra"*). Goods came by head-loads, on cattle backs, and by various types of boats (*cotias* of salt, wheat and rice; almadias of fish, jackfruits, melons, and cucumbers; *jangadas* of palm leaves, hay, and firewood).[13] An early document recording the *rendas* of the Goa island for the years 1541-42 refers to the *renda dos panos* (excise on cloths) from Balghat. No one could import and sell such cloths without knowledge of the State contractor for such imports.[14] There were regular caravans of merchants moving between Balghat and Goa bringing cottons and variety of other provisions.[15] Fr. Gonçalo Rodrigues, a Jesuit who had been to the court of Adilshah in 1561 wrote about the abundance of wheat, rice and all the merchandise coming from Balghat to Goa.[16] There are no easy details available for the inland trade in Bardez and Salcete before the early seventeenth century. When the Chief Superintendent of Accounts, Francisco Paes, was compiling a *Tombo Geral* (General Register of Revenues) in 1595, he could not come across any papers that could throw light on the revenue dues of that taluka in his department archives. He only found a brief note in Kannada written by Azu Naik, who had been collector of State revenues in Bardez in 50s. His note contained the prevailing customary dues in Bardez.[17] However, better details regarding the inland trade in Bardez and Salcete are available in the information gathered by the Revenue Superintendent Nuno Vaz de Castel Branco in 1619 regarding the traditional tariff in force in Salcete. This tariff known as tariff of Shiva Poy lists 67 items that were taxed at the customs house. It refers to the *boyadas* (oxen caravans) from the Balghat and to cloth, sugar, *gonis* (coir rope), and *tannio* (= cotton thread) from Balghat. Possibly, many items like *cambolins* (coir mantle), *rumales* (cloth for turban or *langoti*), cattle, chicken, etc. were also coming from across the Ghats.[18] Pyrard de Laval, who was in Goa during 1608-10 was "surprised to see so many people entering Goa from Balghat, men as well as women, bringing all sorts of merchandise on horses, oxen, donkeys and other beasts of burden.[19] According to a reference to the late seventeenth century the natives of Bardez owned about four thousand oxen for making trips to Balghat. They would make five to six trips to Balghat during the summer months. Manoel Luis from Parra in Bardez was one of the chief caravan owners with about seventy oxen of his own.[20]

Quite some interesting bits of information regarding the inland trade can be gleaned from frequent protests and complaints of the revenue farmers. Thus, for instance, in 1623 Purssia Shet, the tobacco revenue farmer in Bardez, complained to the Government that some influential persons were bringing tobacco from the mainland in boats as well as by land routes to *Mabussa* hidden in the packages of food provisions during day and night time.[21] In 1666 a veteran State councillor D. Manuel Lobo da Silveira had taken over the contract of salt and grain supplies. It is mentioned in the terms of his contract that he should allow the merchants of Bardez to have sufficient supplies of salt at the cost price for two trips to Balghat. For any additional supplies he could charge his commission. The conditions of contract issued to him contained clauses that did not go down well with many interested parties that were making their own profits on those items. The Jesuits, who controlled a sizable share of Salcete revenues, seem to have been among those who reacted strongly. The Viceroy at the time, Antonio de Mello de Castro, who otherwise also disliked the power of the Jesuits, reported to the Crown that they had their own granaries in Salcete, from where they preferred to sell their produce to the Muslims across the Ghats, without caring for the more urgent local needs.[22] It is around the same time that the Viceroy sent a series of complaints to Portugal against the Jesuit Gonçalo martins who purchased the island of Kumbarjua and had opened his own check-post for goods entering from the mainland. This had apparently affected the revenues of the official State check-post of San Thiago or Banastari.[23]

The dependence of Goa upon the inland or hinterland trade was not only with regard to essential commodities. The Portuguese seaborne trade had come to depend on it in the seventeenth century as a result of their problems with the Dutch in the seas. Cloths and diamonds from the Deccan were brought overland through the Ghat routes. In the north the Talkati ghat led into Alorna. It is mentioned as the most frequented route of oxen caravans coming to Kolval in Bardez. In the same region was also the Rama ghat, and this was used by oxen caravans going to Tivim in Bardez and to Bicholim. In Satari the Chorlem ghat started in Chorlem village and ended at Kelvadi in Sanquelim. It was used by caravans coming into Sanquelim as well as to Tivim. Kelghat began at Talvar village controlled from Bhimgad check-post where duties were collected. It led to Kelil in Satari. Here it bifurcated, one route leading to Sanquelim in the north and the other to Usganv and Ponda. Tinai ghat, also known as Kullem ended in Kullem, and from there the caravans would go to Ponda. Duties were collected both at Tinai and Kullem. Kuvessi ghat began in a village of Supa and led to Ponda. The Volvoy river, and the Ghat pass of Khandepar were the most frequented routes of the oxen caravans and other merchandise coming from Konkan, the Maratha country and jurisdictions of other neighbouring chieftains. There followed the Usganv and Bolkondem passes. Tanari pass in Embarbacem was very narrow and connected with the lands of the Sawants and the Marathas. There was a pass in the Kuvessi ghat. Yet another pass in the Dighi ghat, close to Supa, was used frequently by the Marathas to invade Ponda, Zambaulim and Salcete. This route was much used by the cloth-bringing caravans. There were passes in the Kundal ghat at the extreme end of Embarbacem and almost in Zambaulim. It led via Naikini to Kunkali. Finally the Donkorpem ghat in Verlem of Zambaulim led into Netarli village.[24]

What about the movement of goods through the criss-crossing network of the waterways? The information gathered by Afonso Mexia regarding the customs tariffs of the passages into the city of Goa provides us some indication of goods arriving via the rivers of Tisvaddi. There are other archival references pertaining to later periods and other areas. The records of the revenue farming contracts refer to a *renda grande* (major revenue head). It meant the income from duties charged on supplies that came from Sanquelim and Bicholim (from Sarmandusa till Kundai) through rivers of Narve, Chorão and Penha da França to any of the check-posts surrounding Goa. There was also a *renda pequena* (minor revenue head) or income from duties charged on provisions that came to Goa from the mainland through the river of Rachol in the *almadias* (canoes) of Bandode till Madkai.[25]

There is much correspondence in the books of *Reis Vizinhos* (Neighbouring Kings) of the (HAG) about the salt trade using the Goan waterways. Thus, for instance, in 1678 the authorities in Goa refused permission to the Maratha subhedar of Bicholim to transport salt of Pernem to Manneri through the rivers of Kaissua and Kolval. That same year the Goan authorities agreed to release a vessel belonging to the havaldar of Bicholim caught in the river passage of Narve while carrying without licence rice from Santo Estevão to Bicholim.[27] Two years later the subhedar of Phonda is granted permission to send foodstuffs through the rivers of Goa to Sanquelim and from there to Bhalgat. The permission was granted on condition that the goods would be reported at the checkpost of Banastari and pay dues as fixed.[28] In 1682 the Revenue Council of Goa determined that the *savodos* coming from the Maratha territories to fish in the rivers of Chapora and Aldona should be made to buy salt in Goa instead of buying it in the deposits of Fatorpa and Manneri.[29] Besides salt, Goa had only salted fish, copra and areca to export in exchange for almost everything else it had to import, including rice. Even so the trade with Balghat continued to be important and essential for the survival of Goa in the eighteenth and nineteenth centuries as the pressure of the Marathas mounted and the decline of Goa made it no longer an attraction to the foreign merchants. That explains also the rise of the market centres in Mapusa, Margão and other provincial town or *vilas*.[30]

Rural Crafts and Skills

It can be concluded from the movements of goods overland and through waterways and the coast that the rural economy of Goa was affected by commodity production for the market. This in turn leads us to conclude that the property relations in rural Goa must have also been affected by this economic development.

It is important to grasp the evolution of crafts from the natural economy of the patriarchal agricultural system in which the handicrafts were only a sideline activity that complemented the agricultural needs of the peasant households.[31] As a result of growing monetisation made necessary by sovereigns based in distance and collecting revenue in cash (and this was the case since early times in the Konkan which never had its own politically independent units) there was greater feudalisation and growing inequality in property relations in the countryside. This process contributed to reducing the bulk of the village inhabitants to feudal tenants and introducing greater commodity relations. It was a process that forced many peasant households to pay greater attention, if not exclusive attention, to non-agricultural occupations, and to look beyond the village for buyers. However, this did not give rise as yet to professional artisans producing entirely for market. There was the transitional phase when the artisans were still bound to supply for the needs of the village community and receive full or part remuneration in kind. This is the picture that emerges from the evidence I have produced for Goa in the seventeenth century in my past researches. It is interesting to note there the need for Azosy village to make a two-year contract with the cobbler Braz Fernandes. His remuneration is partly given in the form of *namasy* grant, but he is also to be paid ten *xerafins* in cash in quarterly instalments. What is even more interesting is that the *ganvkars* who get pairs of double-strapped sandals are to pay him one and a half *bargany*, and those who order single-strapped pair one *bargany*.[32] This indicates the stage of disintegration of the traditional village communities of Goa and their diminishing self-sufficiency. Of course, the degree of this disintegration could not have been the same all over Goa. Azosy and villages nearer to Goa were more subject to the process due to greater market opportunities in the city. This must have been the case during the pre-Portuguese times when Goa was already known to the Arabs as an important industrial and commercial centre. It was all the more so under the Portuguese who made Goa commercially important on a wider scale.[33] If this impact of the city of Goa upon the village crafts was not greater, it was for three reasons: 1. The Portuguese (applicable to the earlier rulers as well) did not believe totally in free labour, and they required a certain amount of compulsory work from the natives along the lines of *veth begari*. The Portuguese punishments were also of this kind, thereby providing forced labour in the gunpowder manufactory and the galleys. 2. Large-scale domestic slavery in Goa helped to restrict the opportunities for the natives from the countryside to derive full benefits from the city needs. 3. The large-scale Christianization and the control exercised by the Religious Orders in the village economies was an important factor. We know of skilled labour that had to be lent free of any remuneration to build the new places of worship in the villages,[34] though the majestic buildings in the city and the production of objects of cult invited skills from the Goan countryside despite legislation to keep the Hindu artisans out.[35]

However, what seems to have favoured the growth of greater penetration of the countryside and re-feudalisation under the Portuguese was the all-pervading system of revenue farming and monopolies. This promoted concentration of capital in the hands of some native merchants and their control over the labour they recruited from the villages in connection with their functioning as revenue farmers and their involvement in the city market. It was only the peculiar situation of Goa that did not permit the majority of these Hindu merchants and revenue-farmers to invest in immovable property that saved the villages from facing greater inequality of property relations. [36]

From all the above we can conclude that the monetisation and other factors peculiar to Goa under the Portuguese rule and as their metropolis in the East had brought about the development of a mixed situation of different stages of development of crafts, namely the traditional stage of crafts as a sideline occupation, the next stage as domestic industry that produced for the village community as well as for the market, and also the stage of professional artisans who produced exclusively for the city market and for the developing provincial towns, such as Mapusa and Margão. While the village community records in the seventeenth century continue to describe what appears to be the traditional set-up of village artisans as village servants, there are indications of the disintegration in the fines that are being imposed upon the defaulting artisans, and the fact that these fines are monetary is quite revealing. [37] We also have the description of Linschotten for the late sixteenth century and several other foreign travellers who followed him have left lengthy records of their visit to Goa. The city market they describe could provide every conceivable ware and the native Hindu and Christian artisans were seen as very active in it. [38]

The traditional village crafts were not the same everywhere, though every village seems to have had its *mahars*. Hence, perhaps the saying, *ganv asa thuim marodd asa*. The *mahars* were normally made to live on the frontier of a village, and this could be either because they were regarded as untouchables, or because their presence on the village border helped to ensure the safety of the more important castes on the occasion of the inter-village conflicts. It appears that not all artisans serving a village necessarily lived in that village, and the village *sutar, kumbhar, lohar, mali, dangor, chambar, et al* could be serving more than one village. Some crafts were obviously found in those areas which provided resources for such a craft. Thus for instance the coastal villages and the villages on the river banks had *kharvi, tari,* and *agri* (or *mit-*

gaudde). The villages with palm groves had *bhandari, chauduri,* and *telis*. The other known artisans were *sonar-xett, kansar, ximpi, vollar, modvoll.*[39]

These traditional crafts were organized in their own castes which were endogamous and ensured both the continuity of a craft needed by the community as well as the accumulation of skill through generations of practice in the same family. Afonso de Albuquerque has referred in one of his letters to the guns manufactured by the blacksmiths in Goa, and he describes them as better than those made in Germany.[40] A century later the Viceroy D. Jeronymo d'Azevedo was banning the manufacture of guns in the village of Cuncolim or anywhere in Salcete under penalty of four years in the galleys and even hanging![41] However, even in the other less dangerous occupations the native crafts produced a variety of things required for the functioning of the respective professions as well as for the general use of the people. The carpenters produced the various items of household furniture (which was very simple in the villages) and the agricultural implements of different sorts. The *kharvis* had a variety of nets that were meant for catching different types of fish *(koblem, mag, kanttai, zau, ramponn, kann'ni, paguer,* etc.). There were crafts associated with palm products, supplying brooms, spoons, ropes, coir mattresses, woven leaves, oil, toddy, vinegar, arrack, palm sugar. All these products were widely consumed by the local people and some of them were essential commodities, like the palm oil. Interestingly, caju industry that is so popular today, does not seem to have begun till after the end of the nineteenth century. Garcia de Orta does not refer to the existence of caju in Goa, but we do find reference to the fruit at the end of the sixteenth century. At the end of the seventeenth century Dr. Gemelli Careri describes the taste of caju juice and its medicinal property, but says nothing of any brew of it.[42] Though we have very few details of the various types of products of our native artisans, we are fortunate to have illustrations of quite a few household utensils, agricultural implements, and types of jewellry recorded by Bragança Pereira in his *Etnografia da India Portuguesa*. It is a record of a more recent past, but can be considered as valid in the context of the traditional skills that have changed very slowly in our country.[43]

Many details about the native crafts are available in the records of the Goa city municipality. These records also give an idea of the extent to which the native craftsmen from the surrounding villages were drawn into the city and its commodity-market. The *Treslados das cartas patentes* and the *Registos gerais of the Senado da Camara* (municipal council) in Goa Archives contain licences issued to different types of artisans to practice their craft in the city or to have a shop there. They are first examined and checked for fitness to maintain the standards that are required from a particular craft. These crafts include goldsmiths, gem-cutters, blacksmiths, doctors (*fizica*), shoemakers, slave-retrievers, bleeders, tile-manufacturers, washermen, carpenters, bakers, masons, dyers, barbers, mid-wives, *et al.* We can gather from other accounts that the Hindu doctors (*panditos*) were very popular in Goa and thirty of them were licensed to exercise this profession in the city at any one time. Some of them were given licence to cure only with herbal medicines (*ervas e raizes*). These physicians were granted the privilege of using umbrellas.[44] Incidentally, the licences issued to them were accompained by endorsement of the Church authorities with a clause that they should not practise magic and should require their Christian patients to receive sacraments before treating them.[45]

We are told by Linschoten and Pyrard, who visited Goa in its palmy days, that life was very cheap in the city. Referring to barbers, for instance, we read in Linschoten's account that they could be found "in everie end of the streets... They keepe no shoppes, but for a small money come to mens houses to cut their haires, and make cleane their nails, as well of their feet and hands and also their eares, and their teeth, and to rub their legs and bodies".[46]

We have now many published details about the various market controls in Goa, but the accounts of the travellers and the missionary reports still retain their charm for more vivid impressions of the life conditions in the city. The artisans and various native craftsmen flocked to the city and abandoned their villages in search of better fortunes. Pyrard tells us that crowds of natives pestered the foreign visitors offering to be of assistance, and that they would not mind taking a rap or a kick for earning a small coin. The situation could not have been satisfactory as the city economy was on its downward march as the seventeenth century progressed. For those who had given up their dependance on village economy and had opted for market economy the situation must have been hard and they had begun experiencing the hardship of what we call the capitalist economy. I have referred in *Medieval Goa* to an incident in 1694: A crowd of 500 artisans employed in the State shipyard had been striking outside the residence of the chief superintendent of revenue because they had not been paid their wages for seven consecutive weeks.[47]

I have referred to this aspect of the artisan life as a result of the economic decline of the Portuguese and its repercussions on the fortunes of their Asian metropolis, because it could not but force the native craftsmen either to return to their traditional village set-up or to look elsewhere. Both these things seem to have happened. Firstly, they did not have to exactly return to their home villages, because new market towns seem to have begun evolving in the provinces. Margão and Mapusa, as well as some other provincial capitals came to be classified as vilas.[48] This was a significant development affecting the fortunes of the native crafts and industries. The second effect was the impetus that was given to emigration to Bombay and other places in British India. There was the pull factor of Bombay picking up as *urbs prima* under the British from the early nineteenth century, but there were also the push factors in Goa, other than the general decadence of the Portuguese economy. The Portuguese tendency to overburden with tax all sectors of native economy was an important factor in this respect, particularly the so-called *xenddi* tax on the Hindus. The Hindu artisans and businessmen had to pay this capitation tax at a higher rate than a Hindu peasant.[49]

Agrarian Organization and Praxis

Origin of Village Communities

There were attempts made by the early Portuguese officials and chroniclers to trace the origin of the Goan village communities, but they ended up quoting misty traditions. Afonso Mexia who codified the customary legislation of the village communities in 1526 could only ascertain from learned natives that in remote times four men had cleared the island of Tisvadi and brought it under cultivation. Mexia came to the conclusion that it was impossible to find any more information about the origin of the village communities in Goa.[50] The Portuguese chronicler João de Barros, known for some of the earliest reliable geographical-historical tracts on Asia, traced the origin of the Goan village settlers to some poor immigrants from Kanara who descended the Ghats and reclaimed the land for cultivation. When the soil had been made productive and the population had increased sizably, the territory was overrun by a ruler of Kanara, who allowed the people to continue cultivating their lands in peace, after they had agreed to pay him a fixed annual tribute per village on the basis of joint responsibility of all the original settler-families of each village.[51]

There have been other theories put forward to determine the ethnic origin of the early settlers, and we have already made some references to these right at the beginning of this essay. There is also the tradition recorded in the *Skanda Purana* that refers to the migration of the Saraswat Brahmins form Bengal-Bihar region c. 4th century A.D. The late D.D. Kosambi has upheld this tradition with arguments drawn from religion, linguistics and ethnology.[52] According to another scholarly opinion, the Senvi Saraswat Brahmins of Goa may have come from the Kutch-Saurashtra region some time around the 8th century A.D., probably pushed by the Arab invasions.[53] From wherever they may have come, the Brahmins controlled the best lands of the territory along the upper courses of the rivers in the valleys, leaving the villages along the coast and estuaries to the *chardo* caste members, and a couple of villages to *shudra* administration. They also had the upper hand in the rural administration at the *desa* level. The Brahmin was an essential adjunct of the State in reducing the mechanism of violence; his preaching of submission reduced the total administrative cost. He was also a pioneer into the wild territory, the main instrument of agricultural settlement with his knowledge of calender, new seeds, crops, cattle-breeding, land reclamation and irrigation, etc. all of which had to precede any use of the plough.[54] Their stronghold over the rulers and the *charde* (or local *kshatriya* caste) may be concluded from the many *satikals* and *viragals* in Goa. Most of these depict *Shiva-linga* in one of the upper panels, manifesting strong influence of Shaivism between the tenth and the thirteenth centuries.[55] As Kosambi suggests, the practice of sati served to enhance the prestige of the feudal nobility under the ritual control of Brahminism. Their actual control went far beyond ritualism as we have already seen. Also, each *desa* had a general assembly with representatives of the villages in the taluka. This representation was assigned by tradition to certain villages of every taluka. Thus, there were nine chief villages sending *desais* in Bardez, eight in Tisvadi, and twelve in Salcete. Each of these villages were entitled to send one or two representatives, again depending upon custom. However, out of a total of 29 chief villages in the Old Conquests talukas, seventeen controlled exclusively by the Brahmins were represented in the *desa* assemblies.[56]

Property Relations

All lands were included within one village or another. The village called **ganv** (derived from Sanskrit *gramma*, meaning “aggregate”), was an aggregate of family holdings. The lands were cultivated, non-cultivated and waste. The village community was organised on the principle of hereditary rights in land. The ancient Hindu system of joint family property was its basis. It was a sort of landed oligarchy organized into *vangad* or clans of the original settlers of the village. The *vangad* respected a traditional hierarchy among themselves. Possibly this gradation was based on the chronological order of settlement, or also on the importance of contribution made in the first stages of settlement in some cases. The most respected elder or elders of each *vangad* attended the *ganvpan* or village council, whenever this was summoned by the village clerk (*kulkarni*) through an announcement made by the village *parpati*. Unlike in Maharashtra, a village had no single headman or *patil*, but among the various heads of the different *vangad*, the seniormost was regarded as chief *ganvkar* and had certain social privileges. Thus, at the approach of the rainy season, when the houses had to be protected with palm leaves, the work had to begin on the house of the chief *ganvkar*. Also, at any festive gathering the chief *ganvkar* had to be honoured first with betel and pachodi. At the sowing and harvesting season, the first field to be taken in hands was that of the chief *ganvkar*. The dancing girls had also to perform first before the house of the chief *ganvkar*. However, beyond such privileges he had no other special powers. The administration was conducted with *nem* or consensus decisions of the entire village council.

As already stated earlier the *ganvkars* regarded themselves as the rightful owners of all village lands. Their position corresponded to the *mirasdars* in Maharashtra or *khudkasht* category under Mughal administration. The *ganvkars* alone had a say in decision-making, and any single *ganvkar* could veto a decision if he so wished. However, ordinarily the wisdom of the elders carried the day. By way of exception, some non-ganvkars were also listened to, but had no right to vote. Such non-*ganvkars* were the *kulacari* and the *vantely*. The *kulacari* were like the *upri* tenants-at-will in Maharashtra. A *vantely* was generally an outsider to the village, but whose special skills were utilised by the village. Most commonly required skill was connected with dyke building and repairing in the villages having *khazan* (reclaimed) lands. There were some cases in which the *vantely* were even granted the rights of full ganvkars, as in Kalangut in Bardez and Raya in Salcete.[57]

The *ganvkars* gathered in *ganvpan* could make grants of lands, thereby expressing what has been sometimes described as some sort of joint-ownership of the village lands. It was rather an expression of joint-responsibility for the payment of the revenue to the State. The *ganvpan* also enjoyed the privilege of pre-emption in case a *ganvkar* or another person wished to sell his property in the village. This right would enable the *ganvkars* to keep any unwanted intruder out of the village. The ganvkars auctioned the best rice fields of the village at regular intervals to the highest bidder. An outsider to the village could bid and take land on lease, but he had to find a *ganvkar* to bid for him and then to stand security for him. The *khazan* lands were generally auctioned to a single person as *khot*, and he then would sublet the plots to others who had to belong to *bhaus*, which had the joint responsibility of maintaining the bunds and dykes requiring cooperative labour. [58]

In case a village as a unit was unable to pay its dues to the State, its rights to exercise the powers of *ganvkars* were suspended until they showed their readiness to resume the obligation of payment. Also, if any individual *ganvkar* absconded to escape payment, a time was to be fixed for his return. If he failed to do so, his heirs were given an opportunity to assume the ownership and the obligations of it. If they declined, the village council could decide to bestow it on whomsoever it wished, provided the beneficiary was willing to pay the arrears and meet future obligations. Only in rare cases of rebellion the entire villages or individual properties of the absconding *ganvkars* were confiscated by the State.

The rights and privileges of the *ganvkars* were inherited by their male descendants. Women were excluded. The tradition also protected the rights of a *ganvkar* even if he had to be punished for any misconduct. All the above rights and privileges were collated by Mexia for administrative purpose. As it could be expected, some information was initially withheld from him. As and when the new information came to the knowledge of the administration, that was incorporated in the Charter issued in 1526.[59]

However, gradually the initial accommodating attitude of the Portuguese authorities gave way to ways that began to disrupt the traditional system in the wake of the Portuguese drive for conversion of the natives to Christianity and the pressures that began to build up as a result of the declining trade fortunes of the Portuguese. We shall come to this process very soon.

For all practical purposes it suited the Portuguese, as it did to the earlier rulers of this territory, to leave the natives to rule themselves according to their traditions, as long as they paid the expected revenues faithfully. From time to time extraordinary demands were also made, and the traditional system was helpful in keeping the administration costs low. Normally the village council took all the administrative decisions pertaining to the village. The meetings of the council were held as needs arose, and they were frequent. They would meet generally at open places where there was shade and a cool atmosphere. Hence, these meetings would often take place under a mango or a banyan tree. When only a few met, the meeting was held in the house of a *ganvkar* or in the Church verandah. Occasionally meetings were called by the chief *thanedar* or by the taluka captain at his office or residence.[60]

The *ganvkars*-in-council always had the village clerk with them to declare the *nem* and to record the proceedings. The office of the clerk (*kulkarni*) was hereditary, but in addition to this so-called *escrivão fatiosim* there was generally a clerk accountant or *senaboga* (*shanbag*) to keep the accounts and the register of lands and revenues. The Portuguese designation for the same was *escrivão corrente.* This category of class was made up of candidates examined and approved by the Revenue Department, and their appointment to a village had to be ratified by the village council of the respective village.[61]

Land Distribution

The land allocation was done on the basis of its location and productivity. The fertile and cultivated plains in the river valleys were reserved partly for the maintenance of the temple and the associated needs of worship (*nelly*), partly for the maintenance of the village servants (*namossy*), and mainly for the sustenance of the village *ganvkars.* These lands were considered as common property of the village and were auctioned from time to time. The revenue derived from these lands was used to pay the tribute demands of the State and to provide for the temple and village functionaries and servants.

The elevated areas of the village were, as a rule, set aside for residential purposes, and these were distributed among the families of the *ganvkars.* Each family could thus have a plot for house and an adjoining area for orchard. Such plots are designated in the village records as *gharbata, ghormanda, kulagar,* or *thikan* when they had coconut or areca plantations in them. These were assigned to village servants or to any individual *ganvkars* or other in permanent lease, and sometimes on temporary basis. Terraced fields used for cultivation of cereals like *nachini* (*eleusine coracona)* were called *molloi* or *morod* and were also given on temporary (*vanty*) or permanent lease (*kutban*).

Highlands were given as permanent rent-free grants (*aforamentos*) in lieu of some service rendered to the village. Besides, there were also common pasture lands.[62]

The auctioning of the paddy fields, which seems to have been done annually according to the Charter of Mexia, was often done triennially later. The auctioning could begin only after the entire village had been informed at least five nights in advance (*pancharatri*) by the village crier (*parpaty*). The highest bidder had to present immediately his sureties in the person of one or more *ganvkars* owning sufficient property, and failing to do so the bidder was liable to pay a fine and the land was re-auctioned. The existing documentation does not suggest lack of cultivable land. The migration of peasants to neighbouring territories was caused by heavy revenue demands and forced recruitment of the natives during frequent wars or threats of war with the neighbouring rulers.[63]

It was customary to check misappropriation of land, and this was done at the time of triennial auctionings, but more systematically every twenty-five years. There were cases of encroachments, and often additional area was obtained through reclamation of river banks (*kantorly*). Such usurpations or illegal reclamations were fined. In the 17th century, if the usurped area was added to a property of fixed rent, the fine consisted of four *lari* for each coconut tree planted and two *lari* for every empty pit area. When cereal-producing lands were usurped, these were confiscated in favour of the village community, and the guilty proprietor would pay a cash fine as well.[64]

The measuring of the fields did not follow a uniform system in all villages. In Tisvadi the paddy fields were measured with the *vanva* cane, similiar to the *kathi* of neighbouring Maharashtra. In Salcete a cane of three varas of five spans each was in use. In terms of cubits it must have measured seven and half cubits.[65]

The land for coconut plantations was measured with a rope. This sort of measure called *rasee* was in use elsewhere in India, and it was equivalent to eighty cubits. Even *Arthasastra* refers to *rajju* as unit of land measurement. It is not clear from our records what was exactly the size of the rope used in Goa, but apparently it varied in length in Salcete and Bardez. The trees were planted in Salcete at a distance of one rope from each other. In Bardez five trees were fitted in an area of one square rope.[66] The Cadastral Survey of Salcete (1622-92) also refers to the cane of 18 cubits (*mãos*) or 36 spans (*palmos*) as measures for palm-groves. There is also a reference to covas (*pits*) as measurement of coconut plantations.[67] The Charter of Mexia (1526) mentions twelve paces as standard distance between two palm trees.[68] However, the Jesuit author of the *Arte Palmarica* (Guide for growing coconut trees) says that the distance between one tree and another should depend on the nature of the terrain, with the more fertile requiring greater distance. He refers to the native tradition of keeping them a *bambu* (nine square cubits) apart from each other.[69]

The arecagroves were measured differently. The smallest unit used was *zambo*, meaning the area occupied by one tree. The largest unit was *kagany*, containing 600 trees. Each *kagany* consisted of four kamby and each *kamby* of four *gida* and two *zambe*. [70]

Land Revenue

The land revenue was fixed for each village. It is not clear when and how the assessment was done. The Portuguese retained the traditional assessment and mode of payment. However, calculating the gross income and the land revenue or *sidau* paid to the State or *diwan*, it appears that the system taken over at the time of the Portuguese conquest was that of *rayarekha* of Vijayanagar, even though the local representatives of Vijayanagar in distant parts of its effective control could enforce their own tribute in addition to what they paid to the capital. As elsewhere in Kanara, the imperial authorities were concerned directly only with the customs revenue of the ports and the tolls on the highways connecting the ports to the imperial city of Vijayanagar. In such a loose regime, a local land revenue administration seems to have been autonomous to a high degree. Hence, whatever rate was fixed seems to have been influenced by collective bargaining.[71] On an average the revenue (*foro*) paid in Goa amounted to about one-fifth of the gross income of the village. The term *dhastudoddo* used in the village records for the annual balance sheet suggests that the prevailing mode of assessment could have been influenced by *hastobud* under the Adil Shahi. The assessment may have been a summary one, on the basis of the ploughs used, or also, as it appears more reasonable from our records that the basis was the amount of seed required for sowing.[72] The revenue of palm-groves was assessed in *tangas brancas* per every 100 trees or fraction thereof. A new palm-grove was exempted from normal rent during the first 25 years, during which not more than one-tenth of the normal rent was demanded. [73]

The job of collecting the revenue in the village was auctioned every year, and one who agreed to exercise it for the least commission had to present his guarantors and act as *potekar* or *sacador*.[74] The collection of the land revenue was traditionally done in monthly or quarterly instalments. The *potekar* was generally a money-lender in the village, and he could begin his job only after the village clerk and a couple of elected *ganvkars* (*louvad*) had prepared the account of dues (*ulvary*) to be collected from the individual tax-payers after deducting whatever the village owed them by way of remuneration for services, or by way of any discount for any theft of coconuts or damage to crops owing to the negligence of the village appointed watchmen (*terlu* or *painy*).[75] Basing on the *adau* or the annual balance sheet, the village clerk had to work out a list of the revenue paying *ganvkars* and submit the total dues to the provincial collector (*recebedor*) before the beginning of the new month. He had to submit the receipts from the *recebedor* to the village clerk for record of the village. In case of delay in collection or payment to the collector because of the negligence of the *potekar*, he had to bear the expenses of any enquiry that the provincial collector might institute by sending his men.[76]

The methods of tax collection were very severe and were dreaded by the poor peasants. The *potekar* would pay for the defaulters, but then with a *kusa* or a notification issued by the village clerk and endorsed by the province collector he would proceed to confiscate the cattle, grain, or any movable goods of the debtor and auction them to cover the dues. In the meantime the debtor could be jailed with the help of the *nayaks* of the *recebedor*. The confiscation was done as per the valuation of goods done by a village *gramavarika* in the presence of the village clerk. Nothing more could be taken than what was required for the satisfaction of the debt. If the goods were not sufficient to cover the dues, those who had stood as sureties at the time of land auctioning were required to compensate.[77]

The *potekar* was entitled to collect interest on the money he paid for tax-defaulters. This was known as *bhatkado* when collected in grain, and *narlmodo* when collected in form of coconuts. The rate of interest varied at different times of the year, and the highest rate was probably charged for the months when the rice supply was most scarce. The average rate in the seventeenth century was approximately 11%, but reduction was made in times of natural calamities. The collection of interest was done along with the sixth and the twelfth instalments of rent payable at the time of the harvest. No cultivator could lift any paddy or cereals from the fields without presenting to the watchman a tax payment receipt issued by the *potekar*.[78]

The village customs provided measures to be taken against any *potekar* who exceeded his powers. If a wrong person was arrested by the *nayaks* of the *recebedor*, the potekar was obliged to pay the aggrieved party for each day of imprisonment. Also, if cattle was taken by mistake from a non-debtor, then various rates of indemnity were fixed, depending upon the kind of cattle-head that was lost to its rightful owner. In the seventeenth century four *varaha* were paid for loss of an ox, three for a cow, two and half for a he-buffalo, five for a she-buffalo, and two for a calf. In *xerafins* the rates were eight for an ox or a milk-giving cow, five for a buffalo, and ten for a milk-giving buffalo.[79]

There were provisions to prevent the *potekar* from collecting more cash than he was entitled to. For any reported collection in excess of six *zoitole* he could be made to pay one and half *xerafim* to the aggrieved party. If the excess collection was less than six *zoitole*, the defrauded party would receive compensation by auctioning some goods of the *potekar*.[80] Such provisions in detail seem to imply the tendency of *potekars* to collect more than the legitimate dues from the tax-payers, and it does appear from the records that the *potekar was* a dreaded person. A few illustrations drawn from Kortaly village in 1631 may give us some idea of such extortions: For his inability to pay four *tangas brancas* and five *leais*, John Vaz had one *khandi* and seventeen *kudav* of his paddy auctioned. Diogo Purso owed two *tangas brancas* and one *bargany*, and for that he lost an ox. Francisco Purso could not pay six leais, and his canoe was taken over by the creditor for a month. Another villager owned three *barganya* and one *leal*, and his best cow was auctioned.[81]

Distribution of Profits and Losses

A *dhastudoddo* or balance-sheet was prepared yearly or half-yearly by the *ganvkars* and the village clerk. In the section reserved for *adau* the income from various sources was listed. Chief among them was the revenue from the paddy-fields and the palm-groves. A rather meagre income as derived from the other sources, such as the rent of the village shops, the auctioning of the monopoly rights for growing fish in the *khazan* lands during the months of the year when they were kept flooded, the auctioning of the river passage (*penta*), and so on. The section of expenditure was called *vechu*, and this included among the other heads the *sidau* (*foro*) payable to the State as quit-rents. Then followed the stipends and perquisites of the local functionaries and village servants, as well as the expenditure on religious cult and the public utilities. If the village had acquired any loans, these were also paid off at this time after deducting all expenses from the total income. Whatever remained as balance was shared by the *ganvkars* and some other entitled to it as *jon*. If the expenses exceeded the income, the loss was also shared *pro rata* by the *jonkars* and *khuntkars* (share holders). Thus, for instance, the *dhastudodo* of Azosy in 1669 showed *adau* of 95 *tangas brancas*, 2 *barganys* and 14 *leaes*, but the *vechu* amounted to 1903 *tangas brancas* and 14 *leaes*. The deficit of 307-2-00 was distributed equally among the *jonkars* and each one had to pay 4-1-01. Such deficit situations were more frequent from the second half of the seventeenth century, when the State demands on the villages to meet te cost of defence kept on increasing.[82]

Jon was the privilege of every male *ganvkar* after reaching a certain age, which varied from village to village and was fixed by custom. Every *ganvkar* was very conscious of this privilege, and many of them who had migrated from Goa, would come from time to time to collect their *jon* in Goa. The right for *jon* did not imply the obligation to contribute towards the losses. However, if a *ganvkar* was unable to pay his taxes, his right for *jon* could be auctioned by the village. This could be done only for the life-time of the debtor-*ganvkar*. Already in the beginning of the seventeenth century the indebtedness of many *ganvkars* had led them to sell their *jon* to creditors, and these were often outsiders to the village. Such situations were manifesting new conflicts that were going to disturb the village economy during the years to follow.[83]

The distribution of the *jon* followed different patterns in different places. In some villages the distribution was done *per stirpes*, that is, into as many equal portions as the number of clans or *vangad* in the village community. The share of each individual *ganvkar* then depended upon the number of members in each *vangad*. The custom followed in other villages was to distribute the *jon*. Quite often the village clerk, widows, orphans, and some caste of village servants were granted full or fractional *jon*. Thus, for instance, the *sudras* of Moira were granted a quarter of jon for assisting the wives of the Brahmin *ganvkars* in delivery. It was not unusual to grant a permanent *jon* to the patron saint of the village. The records refer to it as *jono fatiosim*.[84]

Village Functionaries and Servants

There were several village functionaries and servants to help the village in its administration. Whenever the village was required to supply free labour to the State, the village would elect a couple of *gramavarika* to make the necessary arrangements and to lead a batch of workers. The function of a *gramavarika* was also to act as an assessing officer in case of thefts or damage caused by cattle to crops. In some villages such officials were known as *chaugule*, *modestu*, or *kumer*. The chief *chaugula* was generally appointed by inviting bidders for the post. One selected would then present his *gadelikars* or assistants. A *chaugula* was expected to be fair in his decisions and had to be available whenever required by the people. A *chaugula* was liable to be fined if he failed to answer a call.[85]

The village also farmed out the office of the *terlu*, whose job was to guard houses, orchards, palm groves and paddy fields of the village. Usually, each *vado* or ward of the village had a chief *terlu* who was responsible to the village. He could employ others to assist him. The duties and stipend was fixed by the village council. *Musara* was paid by each ward to its *terlu*, and perquisites were collected from the proprietors who were the beneficiaries of the service rendered. In Kortaly the *terlu* received six coconuts out of every 100 coconuts plucked, and two *kudav* of paddy from each plot (*zanvo*) of cultivated field or from each *lanço*.[86]

The village council also appointed the *padai* or *padekar* for each ward to pluck coconuts. Only these were entitled to pluck the coconuts in the presence of the *terlu*. In case of any theft, the proprietors had to present before the village clerk the sworn testimony of the *padai* confirming the theft and specifying the loss. Only then the *terlu* was liable to make a compensation. The *padai* was also called upon to help with the measuring rope or rod at the time of *lavni-pavni* or the auctioning of the fields.[87] Not rarely villages appointed solicitors to defend their interests in the courts of law.[88]

Every village had a certain number of servants whose non-agricultural services were essential for the economic self-sufficiency of a village. We come across such services as those of the *thovoi* (carpenter), *vinani* (blacksmith), *dhobi* (washerman), *kumbhar* (potter), *malo* (barber), *mahar* (basket-weaver), *chamar* (cobbler) and *tari* (boat-man). The services of the barber and washerman were almost exclusively of personal attendance, although the barber also acted as acceptable match-maker. The services of the other village servants were more directly associated with the agricultural needs of the village. The carpenter fixed the sluice-gates that protected the *khazan* lands from over-flow of the rivers. He also collaborated with the blacksmith in providing the villages with ploughs, hoes and other agricultural and domestic implements and utensils. The potter supplied clay vessels for home use and for agricultural purposes. The *mahar* manufactured the *gudve* used for watering *vaingan* crops. He also wove mats, baskets and other bamboo products essential for agricultural operations, such as *souvem* (mat for threshing and drying paddy), *supa* (winnowing fan), *varlo* (a basket of 4-cornered bottom), etc. Besides providing the *ganvkars* with footwear, the village cobbler also supplied them thongs for whips and bags for water.

There is very scanty documentary evidence to illustrate the mode of payment to each of the above artisans, or to deduce their relative importance in different villages. Each artisan who served the village had the revenues of *namasy* rent-free land grant for sustenance. Such grants were hereditary and could not be revoked unless the beneficiary consistently failed to provide the service required. The grant could then be transferred to another person who would agree to serve more dutifully.[89]

In addition to the income derived from the *namasy* grant, the artisans also received *musara* in the form of grain from the individual *ganvkar* families that they served. In the case of some artisans, like the cobbler, they received a fixed sum from the village, and the *ganvkars* paid for the personal services received at a concessional rate. Thus, for instance, the *ganvkars* of Azosy village in Tisvadi had made a two-year contract with the cobbler Bras Fernandes to supply sandals to *ganvkars*. The village had set aside a *namasy* plot for him, and in addition to that 10 *xerafins* were paid every year in quarterly instalments. The ganvkars ordering sandals had also to pay the cobbler a limited sum of one and half *bargany* for a pair of single strapped sandals.[90] In the same village the *ganvkars* would give ten kudav of bhat (paddy) to the washerman as his annual *musara*. The washerman was expected to bring the washed clothes on Saturday without fail, so as to enable the *ganvkars* to attend the Sunday liturgy with clean clothes.[91]

All the village servants were welcomed by the *ganvkars* on the occasion of religious feasts in the village and given a share of special sweet rice cakes (*sadna*) that were specially prepared on such occasions.[92]

The village artisans had to make their rounds of the village every week and attend to the needs of the *ganvkars* who might require their assistance. One who failed to do that could be fined for every case of default. Ordinarily the fine did not exceed one *tanga*, but sometimes it could be as high as five *tangas*.[93]

Each village had its cowherds. Depending upon the number of the village cattle heads, there was one cowherd for the entire village or even one for each ward. It looks as if there was one for every eighty cattle heads, and he was paid about one *xerafin* per head of cattle a year.[94] It was the duty of the shepherd to watch the cattle while grazing and to prevent the cattle from straying into cultivated fields. It was customary to impose a fine, say of two *barganys* for each head of cattle that entered cultivated land any one time.[95]

A village also had a goldsmith (*shet*), who pierced the ear-lobes of female children and sometimes of males as well. He provided the villagers with jewellery of gold and silver. He also acted as a shroff and checked the genuineness of currency which the village officials had to collect for payment of revenue. He received special remuneration from the village for this latter service.[96]

Religious Worship and Rural Economy

Religion was quite central to the village life and the predominance of the Brahmins must have made it even more so. An average of four to five temples in each village of Goa suggests a strong religious control of the village life.[97] Every important village activity had to begin and end with offerings to the family and village deities. Religious festivities were also occasions for gathering of fairs which promoted inter-village economy. It is in this context, for instance, that one should analyse the anger and reaction of the dominant class of Cuncolim that killed the Jesuit Acquaviva and his companions in 1583. The Portuguese chronicler Diogo do Couto describes Cuculi (*sic*) as "the leader of rebellions" and its people as "the worst of all villages of Salcete".[98] The prosperity of this village seems to have been derived from its fertile land that had abundant and fresh waters from rivers descending from the New Conquests and cross it before they became brackish in the neighbouring villages nearing the coast.[99] However, the village had other important economic resources. One of these was its permanent *bazar* at the end of more than one caravan route connecting it with the mainland through the Ghats of the Ashthagrahar province. One of these cut through the Donkorpem Ghat and another through the Kundal Ghat, leading to Netarli and Naiquini respectively. Besides these two Ghat passages there was another coming from Dighi Ghat to Veroda via Talvarda. It was frequented by caravans bringing cloths.[100] Cuncolim *bazar* needs to be considered as an important factor in its socio-economic development. In keeping with the traditional fairs connected with temple and religious festivities, also the bazar economy of Cuncolim depended upon its temple and religious celebrations.[101] The destruction of its temples between 1564 and 1566, and the attempts of the Jesuits to establish Christianity in Cuncolim and its satellite villages of Assolna, Velim and Ambelim in 1583 invited the wrath of the dominant native class. It is important to see their hostility to Christianity in terms of threat to their established economic and social privileges connected with the temples and *bazar*. It is not so easy to assign priority to material considerations in the actual practice of religion and the religious feelings connected with it. It is a case comparable to the Portuguese classic claim of seeking souls and spices of India! The people directly connected with the religious worship or responsible for its promotion generally speak more in terms of purely spiritual motivations. However their activities are sustained by the material wherewithal provided by those engaged in economic activities. So also the reactions of the natives of Cuncolim after the destruction of their temple were possibly a mixture of open expressions of spiritual revulsion and less expressed anger over the damage to socio-economic prospects of the dominant groups of the village population. The demolition of the temples implied deprivation of religious and cultural traditions that sustained an established social structure and its underlying economic base. We know it from the comtemporary Jesuit records that the Hindus of Salcete tried to rebuild the temples and were ready to spend much money to do so.[102] This was confirmed in the case of Cuncolim by a stone inscription found in 1971 at the site of the *bazar*. This inscription of 12 lines in Marathi and deciphered as belonging to the year 1579 suggests that a temple of Mahadev was rebuilt by one Vithaldas Vithoji of Kshatriya descent. The inscription says that any Musulman destroying it will incur the sin of the violation of a holy place, and being a Maratha will incur a sin of killing a Brahmin. By reconstructing it a Musulman will have the merit of going on a pilgrimage to Mecca, and a Maratha doing the same will have the merit of a pilgrimage to Kashi. The inclusion of *shapavakya* and benediction for the Musulmans is interpreted as an expression of good treatment that the Hindus usually received from Muslims of Bijapur.[103] Obviously there was no question of curse or benediction for the Christians.

Temples served also as repositories for the village records, and it was in the temple that the children were educated and the adults organized their cultural activities, particularly their *zagor or* dramatic performances.[104] The banyan tree in the vicinity of the temple served as venue for the village council meetings. It was also in the premises of the temple that a final solution was often sought for property disputes or to decide some cases on oath before a deity.[105]

The revenue of some of the best paddy fields or areca-groves was traditionally applied to the expense of the cult and to the maintenance of the temple priests and other servants. Besides, there were other customary contributions in cash and kind that were offered to the temples on different occasions during the course of a year.[106]

The socio-religious pattern of the Goan villages began to experience a revolutionary change on the eve of the arrival of the Society of Jesus in India. Two gentlemen occupying important positions in the Church hierarchy of the Portuguese in Goa had decided that it was time to bring the love of Christ to the Goan natives, and as one of them, Miguel Vaz wrote in a memorandum he submitted to King John III of Portugal: "Let us do this people favour, honour and justice, and let us not give them into the hands of Krishna and Gopu, Brahmins, about whom they were continually complaining. And knowing these two for the great tyrants they are, I for my part hold that people had good reason to complain."[107] This attitude was not surprising as a result of the Reformation spirit that had already engulfed Europe into warring camps. Already much earlier the initial accommodating approach of the Portuguese, who needed support and cooperation of the local Hindu population to destroy the Muslim masters of Goa, had changed considerably. Very soon the Portuguese felt somewhat confident of their power and position, and we can gauge the feelings of Albuquerque towards the natives from the tone of a letter that he wrote to his king on April 1, 1512. It appears that he would not care a hoot if, as a result of his pet-scheme of colonisation through mixed-marriages, the native inhabitants were dispossessed of their lands. He wrote: "If the Portuguese continue to marry and settle down at the present rate, it looks to me that Your Highness may have to drive out the natives of this island and transfer their lands to the Portuguese settlers. These lands are nobody's exclusive patrimony, but they all belong to the King and Lord of the land".[108]

This sort of "wait-and-see" attitude of uneasy accommodation continued for some time. We have the instance of the proclamation issued by the King of Portugal in March 1518. It stated that all lands in the island of Goa were to be distributed among the Portuguese settlers, excepting those that belonged to the native *Christians* before the conquest of Goa! This could be explained as a move to treat the natives as conquered people, but it could also be the result of insufficient information about the local socio-economic organisation, or even caused by misrepresentations by interested parties. The native people must have been quick to respond to such a blunt reversal of promises made to them soon after the Portuguese take-over, because the proclamation was revised within a year, declaring that only the lands that had belonged to Muslims would be given to the Portuguese settlers, and that none of the lands belonging to the *Canarins* would be taken away.[109]

It was to solve the administrative problems arising from complaints sent to the King by different parties that were considered by the *ganvkars* as encroaching upon their traditional rights, that Afonso Mexia in 1526 collated the customary laws governing the village organisation. It came to be known as *Foral de Uzos e Costumes* with 49 clauses, and was adopted as a Charter of rights and privileges of the *ganvkars.*[110] It was a very significant step towards the recognition of the village community tenancy rights, though the Charter retained quite a few features that were introduced by the Muslim rulers and were detrimental to the traditional interests of the villages. The retention of such innovations would be responsible to some extent for the dispossession of the village communities from their lands, which became Crown lands and were also given as grants to private individuals. This happened soon after the conquest of Goa, when the lands that were owned by the Muslim inhabitants of the city and the suburbs were distributed among the Portuguese as revenue-free grants. Since these lands paid revenue to the village communities, that much of amount was discounted fom the village revenue due to the State.[111]

In the wake of the conversion policy of the Portuguese from the early forties of the sixteenth century, and the consequent destruction of the Hindu temples, the lands which the village communities had applied to the maintenance of cult and its ministers and servants were handed over to those entrusted with the Christian churches and promotion of Christianity in violation of the written convention that the lands would remain in the possession of the village communities and that they would only pay an agreed sum for the upkeep of the new cult. [112] Some entire villagers were confiscated in Salcete taluka to punish their rebellious villagers and they were given as grants to certain individuals. Some of these were transferred in course of time to the Society of Jesus, like Assolna, Velim and Ambelim. Cuncolim and Veroda remained and continue legally even today as a *Condado* of the Marquis of Fronteira.[113] In Bardez the villages of Nadora, Pirna and Revora were handed over to a family of Ranes in 1606 to ensure more effective defence of those border areas.[114] Anjuna in Bardez also lost some of its lands as punishment for a rebellion.[115]

In addition to the official action of the State there were also private interests trying to invest their capital in the village lands or just use their influence and power to acquire village lands and administrative rights as *khuntkars*. From the beginning of the seventeenth century this tendency became more marked. The decline of the Portuguese power had begun, and the arrival of north European rivals in the eastern seas made the Portuguese seaborne trade less paying and a more risky enterprise. In this rush for investment in the village lands the white Religious proved to be a serious hinderance to the lay whites, who had to be contented with a poor show as compared to what the organised and concentrated capital of the Religious Orders was achieving. Besides, the Religious had the advantage of their pastoral hold over the villages and they did not mind using their position to promote the material interests of their orders, ostensibly to plant christianity and to sustain if in the new soil. The frustrated anger of the Portuguese laymen took the form of loud denunciations of the clerical success. Thus, for instance, the Portuguese settlers of the Goa city wrote to the King of Portugal in 1603: "If this State of India is lost, it will be solely because of the Society of Jesus.... They are absolute masters of a great part of this island (of Goa). Most of it they have bought, and at this rate there will be no house or palm-grove left which they will not acquire within ten years from now. The Portuguese settlers are finding themselves impoverished, because they have no lands to invest in, and whatever capital they had, they have lost it in the sea. The income which the Fathers derive form their properties in Salcete alone would suffice to maintain all the Religious houses that we have here.[116]

It was in response to repeated complaints of this nature that several laws were enacted to control the establishment of new religious institutions, or to restrict the number of members they could admit, and to check the acquisition of more land properties by the existing ones.[117] The seriousness of the land-grab on the part of Religious Orders is sufficiently testified by the property registers of the various convents that flourished in Goa and Portuguese Asia. Lands were acquired in Goa and in the Province of the North, not just as foundations for the houses the Religious Orders had in Goa, but also for supporting missionary activities abroad. Thus, for instance, the island of Kumbarjua was acquired in 1655 to finance the Moçambique mission of the Jesuits, and there were properties in Salcete which sent revenues to Cochin and Japan.[118] The suppression of the Jesuits in 1759 and of all Religious Orders in 1835 was largely motivated by the growing bankruptcy of the Portuguese State and the eagerness of its political leaders to exploit the discontent of the people regarding the prosperity of the Religious institutions.

Here we have an idea of the assets of the Convents suppressed in 1835:

Rel. Order	Houses	Inmates	Funds	Rent
Franciscans	4	27	94,631-0-00	638-2-30
Dominicans	10	41	—	23,127-1-00
Ref. Franciscans	7	3	86,793-0-00	980-0-00
Augustinians	8	59	72,646-0-00	18,292-1-00
St. Cajetan	1	16	20,838-0-00	2,936-2-30
St. John of God	4	15	19,983-1-40	721-0-00
St. Philip Nery	2	36	65,938-4-00	8,579-0-00
Carmelites	1	23	10,510-0-00	5,074-0-00
Total	37	248	371,340-0-40	60,348-2-00

Source: Capt. J.J.C. Kol, *A General, Statistical, and Historical Report on Portuguese India* (Selections from the Records of the Bombay Government), X, New Series, Bombay 1855.

As a result of conversion drive the economic pressures on the villages were quite intimidating. Hindus were not to be employed in public service. The *Senvi* Brahmins who had traditionally functioned as village *kulkarnis* were to be replaced by capable converts. The converts were also to be preferred as tax farmers, if their bids were as good as those of non-Christians. Hindu artisans could not be employed to produce any objects of Christian worship. Hindu sailors and fishermen could be recruited forcibly to help the State fleets. The traditional laws of inheritance were modified to enable female converts to inherit when a Hindu head of family died without a male heir.[119]

As in case of all legislation, the anti-Hindu legislation was not always enforced with equal zeal and strictness. The Hindus retained enough economic clout to neutralise much of the legislation and the Portuguese administration remained very much dependent on various services of the Hindu community. However, visible change was brought about on the village scenario. Baroque style of Christianity with majestic churches, temples and road-side crosses, and colourful devotions and festivities did much to bring about a new ethos and to add to the growing bankruptcy of the village communities that had to contribute for all that and every other demand of the Portuguese administration in the guise of defence needs. Lands, labour and money were coaxed out of the villages to establish the new religion. It is said at times that the transfer of revenues from old temples to new churches could not make any difference to the village economy. Such an argument tends to forget the fact that the former cult arrangements maintained many families associated with the cult. Under the new dispensation most surplus revenues went to the common pool of the Religious Orders.[120] Besides lands, *confrarias* or pious associations were used for collecting funds, which were not always used for pious works as intended. One has to look at the books of the expenses of the Religious housed in the city of Goa that they were eating well, and had enough money to lend to the village communities and to Hindu businessmen.[121]

Law and Order in Rural Goa

We have already mentioned the role of the religion and temple in helping the maintenance of law and order. As a rule the State authorities intervened only when the local village elders failed to cope with the responsibilities. This intervention was resorted to when the village community had to proceed to an arrest, which it could not do, or when there was any serious bloody incident in the village, or when a dispute was taken by the villagers on their own to the higher authorities.

Most cases were connected with land administration, but even otherwise the village elders had ways of using social pressures to control or deter prospective trouble-makers. The village *terlu* bore the responsibility of guarding land properties and houses against thieves. They also reported to the Captain of the province if there was any stranger living in the village. The watchmen had instructions to arrest anyone moving outdoors after sunset and before sunrise without a lit torch. They had to arrest also the runaway slaves and return them to their masters. The village-appointed watchmen acted as ordinary guardians of law and order in a village. Only exceptionally the village council would have to resort to extraordinary measures. Thus, for instance, the elders of Karbelly village met in secrecy on September 20, 1620 and appointed ten *ganvkars* to capture some mischief makers who were wanted men and had sought shelter in the village.[122]

There are, however, many references in the documents to the quarrelsome nature of the Goan natives and their tendency to have recourse to courts of law for most trivial matters. Due to this the

Portuguese administration had tried keep certain matters reserved to lower levels without further appeal. Certain petty disputes were to be settled by the village *chaugule* and *gramavarik*. That was a system of arbitration. There were also other summary measures adopted. The cases of the natives involving less than three *pardaus* were to be decided verbally by the presidents of the *confrarias* or religious confraternities. It was also determined that the native Christians should not be imprisoned on any flimsy grounds. To refer a case to higher authorities, the contending party was required to deposit at least two hundred *xerafins*. The higher courts of appeal were the taluka *Ouvidor* and the *Relação* (High Court).[123]

Village Communities in the New Conquests

The New Conquests region came under the Portuguese jurisdiction of Goa in the second-half of the eighteenth century. These talukas account for the whole of territory's forests and have only about 27% of the area under agricultural crops. They shared to a large extent the traditional village community system,[124] but it had developed somewhat differently under longer Muslim control and as a result of the peculiar nature of the local politics of the semi-independent Sardessais and Dessais of the region.[125] These had suppressed much of the village autonomy in order to promote their feudal interests. This was particularly true of Sattari, which was the most fertile region of the New Conquests and where the village communities were totally destroyed.[126] Even here the tradition of village autonomy could not be fully wiped out as it appears from the appeal of several *ganvkars* of Sattari in 1824 to the State to restore to them their traditional rights and free them from the violence and extortions of the local Sardesais.[127] But this came at a time when the general atmosphere in Goa was for the suppression of the village communities as a result of the demands for it by an elected Goan representative to the Portuguese Parliament, Constancio Roque da Costa. He was then Assistant Superintendent of the Department (*Intendência*) of Agriculture and was denied the post of Superintendent when it fell vacant.[128] He represented the interests of the native gentry that was doing well and had developed "nativist" feelings that were looked upon with suspicion by the Portuguese officials and settlers (*descendentes*). Most of the leading natives were from Salcete and were actively involved in the debates of the Provincial Congresses propounding liberal views, including economic liberalism of physiocratic type. Francisco Luis Gomes became a notable exponent of this economic liberalism through his *A liberdade da terra e a economia rural da India Portugueza.*[129] However, the ruling colonial interests were represented by the author of the *Brados* (whose role in the elections for sending representatives to the Portuguese Parliament needs to be taken into account to understand this better), and by his native protegé and collaborator, who wrote a corresponding *Defensa.* Behind the scholarly apparatus of these two one should not overlook their political apprehensions. These colonial burẹaucrats decided to oppose the dissolution of the village communities and thereby abort the growing power of the landed gentry and its nationalist ambitions.[130] Instead they did not mind promoting private interests in the colonisation of the New Conquests by forming a *patriotic society for cultivation of waste lands* in 1841.[131] (already active in the form of a patriotic association since 1828) and by allowing foreign interests to come in.[132]

From the 1880s, and particularly in 1904, 1933 and 1961 the Government tried to regulate the functioning of the village communities with fresh rules and codes. However, in the midst of an overall stagnation of the Portuguese economy and the colonial approach, no measures served or were even intended to win the goodwill of the masses of the Goan inhabitants.[133]

REFERENCES AND NOTES

1. V.T. Gune, *Gazetteer of the Union Territory: Goa, Daman and Diu (Gazetteer)*, Pt. I, Panjim, 1979, p. 57.
2. *Ibid.*, pp. 57-58; Nandakumar Kamat, "Cultural Relations of Goa with Gujarat", *Essays in Goan History*, ed. Teotonio R. de Souza, New Delhi, 1989, pp. 1-16.
3. Nandakumar, *op. cit.*, p. 5.
4. L.K. Pitre, "Buddhism in the History of Goa", *Goan Society through the Ages* ed. B.S. Shastry, New Delhi, 1987, pp. 16-24; B.R. Gopal, "Kadamba Patronage to Jainism and Saivism in Goa", *Goa: Cultural Trends*, ed. P.P. Shirodkar, Panjim, 1988, pp. 3-7; P.P. Shirodkar, "Influence of Nath Cult in Goa", *op. cit.*, p. 12.
5. D. D. Kosambi, *An Introduction to the Study of Indian History*, Bombay; Popular Prakashan, 1975, p. 269.
6. *Ibid.*, p. 277.
7. *Ibid.*, pp. 286, 296.
8. P.S.S. Pissurlencar, "Inscrições Pré-Portuguesas de Goa". *O Oriente Português*, no. 22, 1938, pp. 381-460.
9. *Cartas de Afonso de Albuquerque*, I, ed. Bulhão Pato, Lisboa, 1884, pp. 29-65.
10. A. Disney, "The Portuguese Empire in India c. 1550-1650": Some Suggestions for a Less Seaborne, More Landbound Approach to its Socio-Economic History", Indo-Portuguese History: Sources and Problems, ed. John Correia-Afonso, Bombay, 1980.
11. Teotonio R. de Souza, *Medieval Goa* (= MG), New Delhi, 1979, p. 104, no. 2.

12. HAG: *Monções* 12, fl. 124 (14 March 1613); AHU: *India*, Caixa 3 (Jan. 22, 1615); HAG: *Ms* 7865, fl. 64 (11 Nov. 1688). Such impositions in various forms grew in the course of the 17th century and thereafter under the guise of donativos or free contribution.
13. HAG: *Provisões, Alavarás e Regimentos*, II (Cod. 3028), fls 162 ff.
14. J. Wicki, "Mais Documentos de Miguel Vaz Coutinho, primeiro Vigario Geral de Goa", *Studia*, no. 29 (1970), p. 148.
15. R.R.S. Chauhan, "Marketing in Goa during the sixteenth Century", *Goan Society Through the Ages*, ed. B.S. Shastry, New Delhi, 1987, p. 163; HAG: items imported from Balghat, as well as of goods exported from Goa to Balghat in the late 18th century.
16. H. Heras, "Three Catholic Padres at the Court of Adilshah I", Journal of the Bombay Historical Society, 1928, vol. I, nos. 1 & 2, pp. 158-159.
17. HAG: no. 7598, fl. 86v; Pissurlencar, "Tombo da Ilha de Goa e das terras de Salcete e Bardez", *Boletim do Instituto Vasco da Gama*, no. 62, 1945, p. 142.
18. HAG: no. 1160 (*Assentos do Conselho da Fazenda* (ACF), vol. 2, fls. 145-151v (1623)). The first information was gathered in 1619. The details of the tariff have been published by F. X. Fernandes in an Appendix to his *Memória Histórico-Económica das Alfândegas da India Portugueza*, Lisbon, 1989, pp. 77ff.
19. *Viagem de Pyrard de Laval*, Transl. and ed. J.H. da Cunha Rivara, II, Porto, 1944, p. 105.
20. HAG: *Petições Despachadas do Conselho da Fazenda*, I, cod. 1127, fl. 49v.
21. HAG: *ACF*, II, fl. 198.
22. AHU: *India*, Caixa 27, nos. 4, 28.
23. *Ibid.*, Caixa 27, no. 29.
24. *Instrucções com que el-rei D. Jose I mandou passar ao Estado da India no anno de 1774*, ed. Claudio Lagrange Monteiro de Barbuda, Panjim, 1841, pp. 8-19; Teotonio R. de Souza, "Ghat Passes and Ghat Routes in South Konkan" (Paper presented on the occasion of the 301st Punyatithi Seminar on Shivaji at the University of Poona, 9th-10th Feb., 1982), quoting the text of Ajuda Library (Lisbon), Ms. 54-X-20 which completes the list of ghat-routes published by S.N.V. Joshi, *Marathi Rajvathitil Kahi Ghatmarga Chaukya*, Pune, Bharat Itihasa Sanshodaka Mandal, 1954, listing 161 ghat passes.
25. HAG: *Livro de Termos*, cod. 7836, fls. 227-228.
26. HAG: *Reis Vizinhos*, III Cod. 971, fl, 14-14v.
27. *Ibid.*, fl. 10v.
28. HAG: *Cartas e Ordens*. Cod. 2597. fl. 89v.
29. HAG: *Petições Despachadas do Conselho da Fazenda*, I, Cod. 1127, fl. 9.
30. Pissurlencar, *Assentos do Conselho do Estado*, V, pp. 278-279.
31. A.I. Chicherov, *India: Economic Development in the 16th-18th centuries — Outline History of Crafts and Trade*, Moscow, 1974, p. 128ff.
32. *MG*, p. 85.
33. Chicherov, *op. cit.*, p. 135.
34. *MG*, p. 93.
35. *Ibid.*, p. 117.
36. Teotonio R. de Souza, "Mhamai House Records: Indigenous Sources or Indo-Portuguese Historiography", *The Indian Archives*, XXXI, no. 1 (1982), pp. 25-45.
37. HAG: *Assentos da Communidade de Carambolim*, Cod. 10042, fl. 31v; MG, p. 86.

38. *Ibid.*, pp. 117-119, 211.
39. *A. B. de Bragança Pereira, Etnografia da India Portuguesa*, II, Bastora, 1940, pp. 39-46.
40. *Cartas de Affonso de Albuquerque*, ed. Bulhão Pato, Lisboa, 1884, Vol. I, p. 203.
41. J.H. da Cunha Rivara, *Archivo Portuguez-Oriental*, VI, doc. 259.
42. *Indian Travels of Thevenot and Careri*, ed. S.N. Sen, New Delhi, 1949, p. 202; Linschotten, II, pp. 27-29.
43. Bragança Pereira, *op.cit.*, pp. 76-79; Mahendra Chodankar, "Hindu, Christian and Muslim Jewellery in Goa", *Goa: Cultural Trends*, ed. P.P. Shirodkar, Panjim, 1987, pp. 77-93.
44. Linschotten, *Itinerario*, I, p. 230.
45. HAG: Ms 7696, fls. 73v; Ms. 7698, fls. 71v, 72, 174v.
46. Linschotten, *op.cit.*, I, p. 230.
47. *MG*, p. 153.
48. Ponciano de Souza, *Indice Alphabetico, Chronologico e Remissivo da Legislação*, Panjim, 1910.
49. Teotonio R. de Souza, "Xenddi Tax: A Phase in the History of Luso-Hindu Relations in Goa, 1704-1841", *Studies in the Foreign Relations of India* (H.K. Sherwani Felicitation Volume), ed. P.M. Joshi and M.A. Nayeem, Hyderabad, 1975, pp. 462-471.
50. MG, p. 55.
51. Barros, *Década* II, Bk. V, ch. I, pp. 400-401.
52. D.D. Kosambi, *Myth and Reality*, Bombay, 1962, pp. 166-168.
53. G. M. Moraes, "Dr. Jose Gerson da Cunha: Historian from Bombay, 1844-1900", *JRASB*, New Series, vol. 39-40 (1964-5), p. 26.
54. Kosambi, *An Introduction to the Study of Indian History*, p. 313.
55. Gritli V. Mitterwalner, "Testimonials of Heroism: Memorial Stones and Structures", *Goa: Cultural Patterns*, ed. Saryu Doshi, Bombay, Marg Publications, 1984, pp. 41-52.
56. *MG*, pp. 57-58.
57. *Ibid.*, pp. 61-63.
58. *Ibid.*, p. 63.
59. Baden-Powell, B.H., "The Villages of Goa in the Early Sixteenth Century", *JRAS*, 1900, pp. 161-191: Contains the full translation of the Charter with commentary.
60. *MG*, p. 70.
61. *Loc. cit.*
62. F. N. Xavier, *Defensa dos direitos das Gão-carias, Gão-cares e dos seus privilegios*, Panjim, 1856, pp. 7-8.
63. *MG*, pp. 75-76. Cf. also Appendices A-18, A-11, and A-12.
64. *Ibid.*, pp. 76-77; F. N. Xavier, *Collecção das Leis Peculiares das Communidades*, I, doc. 70.
65. *Ibid.*, p. 77: G. Ghantkar, *An Introduction to Goan Records in Halakannada Script*, Margão, 1973, pp. 49-50. A standard size rod was kept in the taluka office in Margão, and the villages had to take their bambus and get them cut to this standard.
66. *MG*, pp. 77, 88 n. 41; HAG: *Foral de Salcete* (1567), fls. 124-4v; *Foral de Bardez* (1647), fls. 185-186.
67. HAG: *Ms.* 7583, fls. 323-324.
68. Clause no. 9.

69. F. N. Xavier, *Bosquejo Historico das Communidades*, Part II, Panjim, 1852, p. 49.
70. G. Faria, "As Medidas Agrarias das Communidades", *O Oriente Portugues*, XVI (1919), pp. 89-91; HAG: *Ms.* 10226 (Kortaly), fl. 97, two gidas and 19.25 *zambe* are referred to as a *visavo* or one-twelfth of three *kagany*, three *gidas* and 13.5 *zambe*.
71. Sanjay Subrahmanyam, "The Portuguese, the Port of Basrur and the Rice Trade, 1600-50", *The Indian Economic and Social History Review*, XXI, no. 4, pp. 433-462.
72. I. Habib, *The Agrarian System of Mughal India*, Bombay, 1963, p. 198, no. 11: *Hast-o-bud* is mentioned as a summary assessment by estimating the total produce of a village after inspecting all the fields, or just by counting the plough. Cf. F. N. Xavier, *op. cit.*, Part I, pp. 10-25: Gives taluka-wise and village-wise tables of seed amounts required for the *kharif (sorod), rabi (vaingan)* and *molloi* cultivation.
73. HAG: *Ms.* 3070, fls. 582, 645. Similar practice known as *istawa* and applicable to new areas brought under cultivation was there in the neighbouring Maratha kingdom; H.K. Sherwani and P. M. Joshi (eds.), *History of Medieval Deccan*, vol. II, Hyderabad, 1974, p. 550.
74. F.N. Xavier, *Collecção das Leis Peculiares das Communidades*, pp. 83-85, 94, 198, 201-202. 286-288.
75. *MG*, p. 79; HAG: no. 10227, fl. 26 (1630); Ghantkar, *op. cit.*, p. 32, doc. 10.
76. *MG*, p. 79.
77. *Ibid.*, App. 10-A, pp. 252-254.
78. *Ibid.*, p. 80.
79. *Ibid.*, p. 81.
80. *Loc. cit.*
81. HAG: *Ms.* 10226, fls. 10v-11.
82. MG, pp. 82, 256-257; F. N. Xavier, *Bosquejo Historico das Communidades (BHC)*, II, Panjim, 1852, pp. 59, 64ff.
83. *MG*, p. 83.
84. F. N. Xavier, *op. cit.*, I, pp. 62-64; II, pp. 29, 39, 141.
85. HAG: *Ms.* 10045, fl. 32, Ms. 10033, fl. 12.
86. HAG: *Ms.* 10228, fls. 23v-4. The *terlu* received also by way of perquisites 10% of jackfruits, bananas and areca nuts. He received no perquisites if there was a theft. *Cf.* Ghantkar, *op. cit.*, p. 64.
87. HAG: *Ms.* 10204, fls. 23-23v; MG, p. 84, App. A-7.
88. HAG: *Ms.* 10035, fl. 8v; Ms 10038, fl. 15; MG, p. 248.
89. Chicherov, *op. cit.*, pp. 15-43; Baden-Powell, *op. cit.*, p. 268 (clause 12).
90. HAG: *Ms.* 10027, fl. 3v (1666).
91. HAG: *Ms.* 10020, fl. 26v (1608).
92. HAG: *Ms.* 10032, fl. 54v (1667).
93. HAG: *Ms.* 10042, fl. 31v; *Ms.* 10031, fls. 3, 7. A very high fine of 10 *tangas brancas* was established by the *ganvkars* of Azosy in 1672 against the village barber who had become very negligent in his duty. It is said that he was drunk most of the time and was using blunt tools.
94. HAG: Ms. 10022, fl. 13; F. N. Xavier, *Collecção das Leis Peculiares das Communidades*, I, docs. 115, 117, 120.
95. HAG: Ms. 10058. fls. 21v, 23, 27v.
96. HAG: Ms. 10037, fl. 10.

97. Pissurlencar (ed.)., *Tombo da Ilha de Goa e das Terras de Salcete e Bardes*, Bastora, 1952, pp. 163ff.
98. Diogo do Couto, *Década*, vol. X, Pt. 1, Bk. 3, ch. 16, Lisbon, 1788, pp. 383-385.
99. XCHR: *J. N. da Fonseca Papers*: Contains replies sent by various villages and other State bodies to a questionnaire circulated by Dr. J.N. da Fonseca in 1875 with the help of J.H. da Cunha Rivara. These replies were partly used by Dr. Fonseca in preparation of his classic *An Historical and Archaeological Sketch of the City of Goa*, Bombay, 1878.
100. *Cf. supra.* no. 24.
101. *Ibid.*, p. 920.
102. *Documenta Indica*, vol. 12, ed. J. Wicki, Rome, 1972, pp. 916-933.
103. V. T. Gune, "Meaning of "Maratha Houni", *Maratha History Seminar Papers*, ed. A.G. Pawar, Kolhapur, 1971, pp. 1-6; K.M. Bhadri, " A Marathi Inscription from Kunkali", *Sri Venkateswara University Oriental Journal* (Tirupati), vols. 21-22, Jan-Dec., 1978-79, pp. 27-29.
104. HAG: Ms. 10045, fl. 10; Cunha Rivara, *Archivo Portuguez-Oriental*, vol. 4, p. 251.
105. Baden-Powell, *op. cit.*, p. 273.
106. *O Gabinete Literario das Fontainhas*, ed. F.N. Xavier, II, p. 73, no. 1; HAG: Mss 3070, 3071, *passim*.
107. *Documenta Indica*, I, Rome, 1948, pp. 68, 70.
108. A. Baião, *Afonso de Albuquerque: Cartas para el-rei D. Manuel* I, Lisbon, 1942, p. 74.
109. F.N. Xavier, *O Gabinete Litterario*, II, 1947, pp. 94-98.
110. F.N. Xavier, *Collecção das Leis Peculiares das Communidades*, I, doc. 1, pp. 1-15. Has published the full text of the Foral from the original in *Monções* of the (HAG).
111. *BHC*, II, p. 10.
112. *Ibid.*, pp. 11-16.
113. *Ibid.*, II, pp. 28-29, nos. 110, 134.
114. HAG: *Assentos do Conselho da Fazenda*, V, fls. 66-67; BHC, II, p. 61, no. 336.
115. HAG: ACF, IX, fl. 31v; L. Rocha, *As Confrarias de Goa*, Lisbon, 1973, p. 424, no. 133.
116. Cunha Rivara, *Archivo Portuguez-Oriental*, I, Pt. 2, Panjim, 1876, doc. 10, p. 128.
117. *MG*, p. 87, no. 19.
118. HAG: Mss 824, 830, 3026, 3029, 3038, 3041 are some of the codices belonging to a long series entitled *Papers of the Suppressed Convents* that can be usfully consulted to get an idea of the land-grab of the Religious Orders. Cf. also HAG: *Monções* 19C, fls. 734v-736v; no. 2439 (*Diversas Contas*, 1655-1836), fls. 195-203; *ACF*, IV, fls. 109v-110v; Charles J. Borges, *Economics of Goa Jesuits* (1542-1759), unpublished Ph.D thesis, Bombay University, 1989, contains abundant details on the subject of Jesuit properties in Goa. Also provides information about the archival sources where more information may be obtained; F.N. Xavier, BHC (1852), II, p. 29, n. 110: "Os factos porém attestam que os Jesuitas, lançando mão de todos os meios repugnantes à razão , ao direito da propriedade, e ao seu instituto, conseguiram, por meio de confisco desapossar as communidades das ditas Aldeas ..."(refers to Assolna, Velim and Ambelim).
119. *MG*, p. 93.
120. *BHC*, II, pp. 123ff., 153ff. Much detailed and tabulated information about the

contribution of individual villages for the building and maintenance of churches and the cult. Cf. A.R. Kulkarni, "Marathi Records on Village Communities in Goa Archives", *The Indian Economic and Social History Review*, vol. IX, nos. 3-4, pp. 377-385: The temple servants are listed as *joshi* (Brahmin priest), *bhavin* (menial servant), *devali* (brother of bhavin), *kalavantin* (dancer), *ghadi* (soothsayer, generally of *Shudra* caste), *gurav* (non-vedic priest), *bhagat* (dealer with demons), *jalmi* (person performing rituals in the field).

121. Teotonio R. de Souza, "The Voiceless in Goan Historiography" *Indo-Portuguese History: Sources and Problems*, ed. John Correia-Afonso, Bombay, 1981, pp. 114-131, pp. 227-243; *BHC*, II, p. 156: Refers to parish priests who use parish funds for helping nephews and nieces.
122. HAG: Ms. 10056, fl. 43v.
123. MG, pp. 100-101.
124. A.R. Kulkarni, "Portuguese in the Deccan Politics: A Study of New Marathi Documents from Lisbon", *Indo-Portuguese History: Old Issues New Questions*, ed. Teotonio R. de Souza, Delhi, 1985, pp. 28-33.
125. J. H. de Cunha Rivara, *Brados a favor das comunidades das aldeas do Estado da India*, Panjim, 1870, pp. 35, 50; Teotonio R. de Souza, "The Ranes of Sanquelim", *Goa Today*, March 1987, pp. 114-122.
126. *Boletim do Governo*, no. 42 (1852); F. X. E. Fernandes, *India Portuguesa: Estudos economico-sociaes*, Bastora, 1905, pp. 84ff.
127. F. N. Xavier, *Defensa*, pp. 49ff.
128. F. N. Xavier, *Collecção de Bandos*, 2 vols., Panjim, 1840-1850, contain valuable transcripts of legislation and information about the New Conquests. Unfortunately, very little use has been made by scholars and administrators of these precious volumes.
129. F. L. Gomes, *A liberdade da terra e a economica rural da India Portugueza*, Lisbon, 1862.
130. Mariano Dias, "Fr. Caetano Vitorino de Faria", *Essays in Goan History*, ed. Teotonio R. de Souza, Delhi, 1989, pp. 139-154.
131. F. X. Xavier, Bandos, I, pp. xix-xx, 219-224.
132. F. X. E. Fernandes, *op.cit.*, p. 89: Gives details of the land held by six foreign nationals. The experiment of plantation seems to have been short-lived. This experiment had provoked the ire of the Ranes who saw in it a challenge and threat to their feudal rights. Cf. also *Relatorio da Commissão encarregada de demarcar os terrenos da Provincia de Satary*, Part 3, Panjim, 1869, pp. 50-55.
133. For good summary surveys of village communities of Goa with historical and statistical details, *Cf. Report of the Goa Land Reforms Commission* (popularly known as Dias Report after its Chairman A. L. Dias, I.C.S.), Panjim, 1964; *Techno-Economic Survey of Goa, Daman and Diu*, New Delhi, NCAER, 1964; and J.C. Almeida, *Aspects of the Agricultural Activity in Goa, Daman and Diu*, Panjim, 1967.

[Reprinted from *Goa Through the Ages*, II, ed. Teotonio R. de Souza, New Delhi, Concept, 1989, pp. 78-116]

2

THE VOICELESS IN GOAN HISTORY
(A case for the source-value of the Church records)

It is important to bring about a radical shift in the trend of Goan historiography to make it relevant in the context of its new liberated status and of the new prospects and challenges which this change has laid before us. Such a shift of trend is conceived here in terms of a reinterpretation of the Goan past by replacing the myth of 'Golden Goa' with the reality of the socio-economic pressures as well as opportunities to which the Goan population was introduced by the Portuguese rule.[1] This proposal of a new purpose-oriented historiography may not appeal to those who are contented with the sight of some patches of exotic cultural vestiges left behind by colonial rule. I cannot resist the temptation of quoting for the benefit of their taste from the chapter on 'Golden Goa' in Maurice Collis' *The Land of the Great Image:* 'For Latins the city was a paradise, a lotus-eating island of the blest, where you could sit on your veranda listening to music as the breeze blew in from the sea, *with humble folk within call to minister to your every wish' (emphasis added).* No wonder it was called Golden.[2] The author could not have been more sarcastic in his condemnation of a history of a colonized people from the stand-point of a colonial power.

There is an abundance of published historical works on Goa,[3] but a critical look at them leaves us with hardly anything that has any depth of analsyis and is not tainted directly or indirectly with the myth of 'Golden Goa' and its implied theory of welfare that served to quieten the guilt of the erstwhile rulers and few local beneficiaries. Much of this bibliography can be classified as 'tourist brochure history', seeking to focus the stage-lights upon some surface attractions, leaving thereby in the dark some stark realities which need to be considered also as a part of the same colonial legacy. One could draw up a long list of such grim problems facing the Goan population in the wake of its liberation, but let me point out only our democratic but communalism-infected politics, and our strong and liturgically alert Christian minority in a state of economic and political lethargy.[4]

There is another attitude also that can be detected in many of the existing historical works on Goa. It tends to regard colonial rule as *gesta Dei per lusitanos*, that is, God working through the Portuguese. Diogo do Couto, for instance, even after a harsh commentary on the Portuguese administrative abuses and military failures, ends his *Diálogo do Soldado Prático* by repeating in the fashion of the previous chroniclers that the presence of the Portuguese in the East was by divine dispensation. [5] We are not surprised also with the attitude of the well-known early and late missionary historians from Europe. They chose to write in terms of 'spiritual conquests', which justified the material conquests of Portuguese arms. But what can surprise a Goan historian following our new trend is the fact that he does not need to work hard to find illustrations of the maxim 'more popish than the pope'. To quote one man of the soil for producing a reactionary document in Portuguese, we have Sebastião do Rego who was admitted into the Theatine Congregation. He preached a sermon in 1744 describing the Portuguese as sent by God to India to be 'the new Peters and Pauls chosen to exalt the holy name of Christ'.[6] This may sound old history, but a more recent Goan author who studied the recruitment of native clergy in India has described the opening up of certain Religious Congregations to natives of Goa as a result of the fact that 'almost three centuries of Christianity and Christian influence had made them better men', [7] meaning I suppose that they had learnt to sing the desired tune.

I wish to distinguish yet a third category in the existing bibliography on the history of Goa. It covers the published documentation. We have present among us here the venerable figures of Rev. Dr. J. Wicki, S.J. and Rev. Dr A. da Silva Rego, who have given us their best in their monumental series of published documentation entitled *Documenta Indica* in 18 vols. and *Documentação para a História das Missões do Padroado Português na India* in 12 vols. Their work may appear to be of usefulness only to the historians of Christianity in India, but there is much in it for writing the kind of history I am advocating here. I wish to recall in this connection the influence that J.H. da Cunha Rivara, who arrived as Chief Secretary of the Goa Government in 1855 and let himself stay here for nearly twenty years, had on the study of Goan cultural institutions.[8] This scholar-administrator showed great concern for the preservation of Goan language and Goan village communities. There followed a spurt in historical research under his patronage and quite a few bright young Goans began delving into the Goan past. No one who wishes to study the socio-economic history of Goa will be grateful enough for the documentation contained in F.N. Xavier's *Collecção das Leis Peculiares das Communidades, Bosquejo Historico das Communidades,* and *Collecção de Bandos*, not to mention his several other publications.[9] Even though the author lived in an atmosphere of comparative constitutional freedom the official protectionism did not permit him to do more than compile objective information. There is no attempt at interpreting these data and the author has a very simplistic explanation for this in a note appended to Part Two of the first edition of his *Bosquejo*: 'I have not taken upon myself the task of presenting my reflections upon the content of the documents published herein, not only because it would be alien to my intended goal, but also due to my lack of sufficient strength to do it." [10]

We cannot bypass the commendable work done by the former Director of the Historical Archives of Goa (HAG), the late Prof. Pissurlencar. I wish to choose, however, to comment only on his *Agentes da Diplomacia Portuguesa na India*, which may be regarded from among all his other publications as most relevant for studying the native response to Portuguese rule.[11] Whatever may have been the intentions of the author in the post-Republican era, this work of his could prove very conclusively to his Portuguese masters that, contrary to the prevailing belief, the Hindu community of Goa had served the Portuguese colonial and political interests with unremitting constancy and zeal. This truth may give little comfort to those who are making political capital today out of their little knowledge of the past.

To conclude this sketchy evaluation of the past trends I may still have to refer to the works produced in the past few decades. We have a veteran of the Portuguese imperial history, and it would be highly presumptuous on my part to apply shorthand to his vast stock of writings. I feel overawed by the vast erudition and the catchy literary style that we see in C.R. Boxer's writings, but perhaps I shall only make one remark, and that is, there was one group among the Goan natives that had caught the eye of the Portuguese (shall I say 'more than the eye'?) and that seems to have been the only group that has so far attracted the attention of Prof. Boxer as well. The solution to the riddle will be found by those who are familiar with his studies on 'Portuguese fidalgos'. [12]

As to other historical works of this period, they try to do justice to the native people, but often there is too much political passion in them, reducing greatly the desirable historical objectivity based on sufficiently wide and accurate documentary evidence. There are surely some praiseworthy exceptions, and among these I would place B.G. D'Souza's *Goan Society in Transition*. However, it being a doctoral dissertation in sociology, the author's approach takes him more into generalisations valid for medieval Indian society as a whole, rather than into concrete details of the life-conditions of Goan society.[13]

The Portuguese official chronicles and State papers are of little help, and we find A.C. Teixeira de Aragão voicing this deficiency in Indo-Portuguese historiography: 'Past historians who wrote on Portuguese India cared to describe only the military feats of the Portuguese and the efforts spent in spreading Christianity. Mighty little has been done to describe the usages, customs, and nature of the natives, the civilizing influence of our rule, the institutions, privileges, and economic administration, and all that characterised the social relations between the rulers, and the ruled'.[14] The documents which he culled from various archival repositories, including the (HAG), and published in the third volume of his *Descripção Geral e Histórica* das Moedas are surely a great help to study the market economy that directly affected the economy of the capital city of Goa, and only indirectly the outlying jurisdiction. However, these records do not help us to form more than a vague idea of how the monetary policies of the Portuguese affected the daily life of the rural inhabitants. All that one can conjecture is some sort of impact upon the sale of the surplus products of the countryside in the city market, as well as upon the tax-revenue collected from the countryside by the central administration. We have luckily well preserved city municipality records as well as records of the village communities to provide more detailed information that can take us closer to the common man's reality in his rural setting.[15] But we also have valuable Church records that can help us in this task. It was the new religion that brought the colonial presence of the Portuguese in closest possible contact with the native population. Let me therefore expose the modalities of this interaction and then proceed to analyse the value of various Church records which have preserved for us accounts of that interaction or data that can be put together to achieve our purpose of resurrecting the history of the people of Goa.

Church Organisation and Activity in Goa

It was only after Goa was made the headquarters of the Portuguese activities in the east that the Church organisation also gained in complexity and importance. It was made suffragan diocese in 1533 and raised to the rank of a metropolitan archdiocese in 1557. Further titles followed in the course of centuries. Hence, from the beginning and at successive stages the Church of Goa was headed by Vicars General, Apostolic Commissaries, Bishops, Archbishops, and Patriarchs. This last title was granted in 1886. They were not necessarily appointed for life, but most of them died in office. A great majority of them belonged to the Religious Orders, generally Franciscans, Augustinians and Dominicans. This was so, because the Religious Orders dominated the missionary field till their suppression in 1834-35.

As we have just said, different Religious Orders had established their missionary headquarters in the capital city of Goa, but of these we need to single out the Jesuits and the Franciscans for the intensity of their labours in the capital and rural areas of Goa. The Dominicans helped somewhat in the island-taluka surrounding the city, but the Jesuits had an exclusive hand in the establishment of the Church in Salcete, and so did the Franciscans in Bardez. The Church of Goa, which had begun with one parish in the capital city, had extended by mid-17th century to form as many parishes as the village communities in the three talukas that made the 'Old Conquests' of Goa.[16]

The expansion, organisation and working of the Church in the parishes was closely linked with the prevailing socio-economic factors. It may be interesting to note that it was the high rate of mortality caused by an epidemic in the city of Goa in 1543 that led to the breaking-up of the original single parish into four.[17] The multiplication of the parishes village-wise also depended upon the number of the faithful and the financial viability of the area to maintain the cult. It may be said in this connection right away that the Portuguese crown was bound by its duties of Crown Patronage to maintain the Church institutions and the cult in the East, but it got the natives not only to pay for these, but even to finance the wars for the survival of the Portuguese presence in the region.[18] In the proceedings of the State Council that voted for the extraction of such *donativos* (euphemism for compulsory payments) we find mentioned time and again that endangering Portuguese rule was tantamount to placing the Christian faith in jeopardy.[19] Returning to our theme of parish-organization there was the caste-division of the society which remained crystallised in the religious confraternities or *confrarias* which played a prominent role in popularising the new cult and in helping it to gain roots in the native soil.[20] It was through these bodies that petty cases of justice were settled in the villages, discouraging thereby the tendency of the natives to sue each other into misery for most trivial reasons. It was again through these bodies that acts of charity were practised towards the destitute of the village, and particularly worth praising were the steps taken in some villages to provide seed loans to peasants in need during the sowing season, saving them thereby from the clutches of the village moneylenders.[21]

It may be asked if opportunity was given to sons of the soil to join in the responsibility of attending to the pastoral needs of their countrymen. More than a required number of natives were trained as secular priests in the training-houses run by the religious, particularly by the Jesuits. However, as long as the religious remained in effective control of the Church in Goa, the natives clerics had to remain contented with subordinate roles. We find cultural prejudices and political insinuations reflected in the reports submitted by the religious to the civil and ecclesiastical authorities in Lisbon and Rome to evade instructions requiring a better deal for the native clerics. The attachment of the religious to their revenue-bringing parishes also played its part in their refusal to hand over the administration of these parishes to the native clerics.[22] Hence, there was much more than just a slip between the legislation of the time and the actual practice. However, the dissatisfaction of the native clergy contributed substantially to building up resistance to Portuguese rule. We have records of grievances sent to Lisbon by the village communities of Goa, and we know that there were native clerics who helped the drafting of these grievances.[23] It is also well known that on more than one occasion the native clerics led movements of public discontent against Portuguese rule.[24] It is sufficient to note here that as a result of the conflict between the sincere needs of the Church and colonial interests there arose an intellectual elite conscious of its rights but with little scope for their fulfilment.

To conclude this section I wish to discuss briefly three other institutions which might be considered secular in their origin, but were manned largely by ecclesiastics or performed very much of religious or spiritual functions. In their order of establishment these were: 1) Father of the Christians; 2) Inquisition; 3) Board of Conscience.

1) Father of the Christians or *Pai dos Cristãos*, as he was called, was generally a Franciscan in Bardez and a Jesuit for the remaining jurisdiction of Goa. His task was to promote conversions to Christianity and to look after the spiritual and material welfare

of the new converts. Dr. Wicki has made available to us in published form the documentation that was available in the (HAG) regarding the activity of the Father of the Christians in Goa. [25] The documentation relating to this institution covers many details of socio-economic nature such as payment of tithes, administration of justice, customs of inheritance, employment of poor and orphan converts, liberation of slaves, and so on.

2) The Inquisition played a formidable role in Goa and has been branded as the worst of all that functioned anywhere in the world.[26] Apart from certain published reports of eye-witnesses and victims, particularly of the French doctor Dellon, all that is left of the documentation of that institution are a few stray files in the National Archives of Lisbon and an inventory book in the same repository giving a complete list of the condemned and acquitted from the time of its inception till 1774.[27] The total number had reached 16,172. It included persons of different nationalities, but nearly three-fourths were Indians almost equally represented by Christians and non-Christians. Many of these Goan natives were hauled up for crossing the border and cultivating lands in the mainland.[28] The prevailing system of property relations in the village communities of Goa and the ever-increasing burden of Portuguese taxation left no other alternative to many Goan peasants but to leave their homes and go to cultivate land in neighbouring Muslim lands. The Inquisition watched over the purity of faith but did not suggest anything constructive to remedy the economic distress of the social groups which had no say in the administrative structure of the villages.

3) The Board of Conscience or *Meza da Consciencia* was not exactly a distinct institution because it was an activity of the Inquisition itself. It started functioning from the early days of the Inquisition in Goa, but it had ceased to exist when Francisco de Souza wrote his *Oriente Conquistado*. The author tells us sarcastically that being a board of conscience it was bound to be short-lived in India where consciences are upset more easily than stomachs.[29] As we know from the documentation relating to the Inquisition published by A. Baião, there were conflicts between the officials of the Inquisition and the civil authorities, including viceroys, who resented the interference of the Inquisition.[30] However, the Inquisition being an institution of somewhat hybrid nature, neither fully secular nor fully ecclesiastical, it had

apparently won the confidence of the natives. Besides, Lisbon consistenly took serious note of the reports that went from the Inquisition.[31] We read in a memorandum sent by the general assembly of the village communities of Salcete to the Crown in 1643: 'It is impossible for the people of this land to find justice, because their enemies are too powerful... We request that the officials of the Holy Inquisition be entrusted with the task of conducting a secret inquiry into all that has been exposed in this fearing reprisals'. [32] In the appendix to the same memorandum they repeat: 'We request Your Majesty that if any inquiry is instituted it should be entrusted to the Board of Conscience formed by the officials of the Holy Inquisition, because that is the only body that can be trusted with a mission of doing fair justice'. Hence, it is not surprising that the continuance of such a body was irksome to colonial interests.

Source-Value of Church Records in Goa

After reviewing briefly the organisation and activity of the Church in Goa we are now in a position to appreciate the source-value of various records that have survived of this activity. It is not possible for me to present here any exhaustive survey of these records, and all that I shall try to do is to delve into a somewhat detailed analysis of some select records that are available in the Goa State Archives (HAG), in the Patriarchal Archives (PA) and in the parishes.

There are may scattered references to Church activity in the State papers, but however useful they may be for our purpose, I shall limit my attention to those records only which once belonged to the Religious monasteries and were transferred to Government archives following the suppression of the Religious Orders in 1834. The records of the Jesuits had been taken over by the Government even earlier, namely at the time of their suppression in 1759. All these records bound into nearly 400 volumes are still awaiting a scholar who may decide to use them to study the impact of the activity of Religious Orders upon Goan economy. I was able to use these records to draw a graph indicating *price-rates of essential commodities* in 17th century Goa for the purpose of my doctorate dissertation. I could do it with the help of the day-to-day accounts showing item-wise income and expenditure of the religious houses. Unfortunately there are no such account books for the period prior to the 17th century, and even these are more or less complete only for the Augustinian monastery of Our Lady of Grace. These same ledger books can also provide information regarding employment and wages of artisan and menial labour in service of the religious. One gets even such interesting details as the cost for extracting a tooth,[33] or the reward paid to a slave retriever to get a slave back.[34] The same account books and the books containing the title-deeds of landed properties can help us to study the impact of the concentrated capital of the Religious Orders. Their capital came partly from endowments and legacies, but it was also to a large extent reproduced through investment in trade and through industrious methods of farming. Trading in real sense was banned for the Religious, but they always explained their activity as exchanging the surplus of their various mission posts. However, there is documentary evidence to show that whatever exchanging was going on it did not always differ much from trading.[35] But the very fact that the religious could not very openly and intensely indulge themselves in trading, their accumulated capital began disturbing the rural economy of Goa long before the decline of the Portuguese Goa-based seaborne trade forced the lay Portuguese settlers to seek safer investment in village lands. However, the latter were no match against the spiritual control and the concentrated capital of the religious, and this frustration of the lay settlers can be seen reflected in the constant complaints to the Crown. The municipal councillors were writing to Lisbon in 1603: 'If this State of India is lost, it will be solely because of the Society of Jesus.... They are absolute master of a great part of this island, most of which they have purchased, and at this rate there will be no house or palm-grove left which will not be theirs within ten years from hence. The Portuguese settlers find themselves impoverished, because they have no lands to invest in, and whatever capital they had they have lost it in the sea. The income which the Fathers derive from their properties in Salcete alone should be sufficient to support all the religious houses that we have here'.[36]

The success of the religious in farming excited much jealousy of the lay Portuguese settlers. The Jesuits in particular had more than doubled the output of their lands through their more rational approach to cultivation. We know, for instance, that the three villages of Assolna, Velim and Ambelim were valued in 1578 at 2,010 xerafins. They were then given as a grant to the Jesuits. By 1635 their yield was assessed at 5,500 xerafins.[37] The consolidated plot and large palm-groves of the religious also gave rise to a type of bonded labour known as *mundkars*, who were bound to the land as a result of small loans which they could hardly repay.[38] There were indications that the religious were benevolent to their *mundkars*,[39] but the lot of these must have taken an unhappy turn when the suppression of the Religious Orders pushed them into the hands of new secular landlords.

In addition to what I have said about the impact of the accumulated moneys of the religious, the papers of the suppressed convents also yield information regarding *loans, rate of interest,* and *the nature of goods pawned.* An inventory made of all the moneys and properties of the various houses of the Society of Jesus in the Portuguese East in 1759 shows that five houses in Goa alone had given out loans worth over 3,50,000 *xerafins*. Their major customers were the general assemblies of the village communities and also some individual village communities, which mortgaged their lands against these loans to satisfy the exactions of the State. The general assembly of Bardez had borrowed 1,00,000 *xerafins* from the Professed House of Bom Jesus at an interest of 5%, while the general assembly of the Salcete villages had taken a loan of 62,200 *xerafins* form the same house for 6% interest. It is interesting to note that the Jesuits, who have been maligned for being religious fanatics and champions of the anti-Hindu drive in Goa, had given 23,800 *xerafins* as loans to several Hindus residing in Kumbarjua.[40]

To conclude my presentation of the Church records in Goa archives I wish to introduce yet another manuscript entitled *Cartas de Alforria aos Escravos*.[41] Slavery had been a common feature in Goa much before it became a profitable trade for the Portuguese in the Americas. Pyrard had left us a vivid and lewd description of the slave market of Goa in the beginning of the 17th century.[42] He also tells us that Goan natives were not enslaved because of a privilege they had secured from the Crown.[43] However, even without such a privilege it would not be easy to enslave Goan natives in their own territory where they could easily escape, and we do not know whether any were included in the West-bound cargoes. But the Public Revenue Department had a resolution passed in 1646 to send as many *corumbins* from Goa as possible to cultivate lands in Ceylon.[44] We do not know in what capacity they were to be sent or whether they were sent at all, but it can be inferred from the manuscript I wish to introduce here that a good number of slaves recorded therein belong to the *corumby* and *chardo* caste groups of Goa.

The manuscript containing 112 folios is a register describing the deeds of obligation drawn by various Fathers of the Christians during the years 1682-1759 and signed by the slave-owners binding themselves to set their slaves free within a maximum time-limit of ten years. This register contains nearly 350 such deeds. A great majority of the slaves were from across Goa's borders as can be inferred from their designa-tions *gatual* and *balagaty*. Nearly two-thirds of these are females of an average age of twenty. Several of these deeds also refer to orphan children handed over by the Fathers of the Christians to the care of certain families under condition of teaching them good manners and the Christian doctrine, treating them well in their infimities, training the boys in some suitable skills, and giving the girls in marriage at the appropriate age.

In the midst of cruelties to which the slaves in Goa were often subjected by their owners, the concern shown by the Church brought them some solace in their sufferings and some hope. It was only in mid-19th century under British pressure and the wave of liberalism in Portugal that slavery was finally abolished, but by then their number had dwindled very considerably, and in 1853 all the three talukas of the Old Conquests of Goa did not have more than 100 slaves. [45]

Church Records in the Patriarchal Archives

It is unfortunate that the bulk of early records from the (PA) is lost to scholars. In response to an order of the home government, the Arch-bishop of Goa Francisco da Assunção e Brito handed them over to be shipped to Portugal in 1775. It is not known where they finally landed.[46] But this does not seem to have been the only occasion when records left the central repository of the Church records in Goa: Archbishop Jose Maria da Silva Torres, who governed the archdiocese during 1844-49, had taken away the records covering the period of his administration for the purpose of writing his autobiography, and we do not know if they ever came back.[47] The bulk of the earliest records that are now available in the (PA) belong to the late 18th century. The consultation becomes tedious due to lack of proper classification and of a systematic inventory of the holdings.

Very useful from among the other records of this repository is a series of codices entitled *Róis da Christandade* (Church Rolls) dating from 1773. They carry yearly certificates issued by the priests in charge of various parishes indicating the total numbers of the faithful and providing various interesting details regarding their age, health, sex, reception of sacraments, employment outside the village, and so on, which are invaluable for a demographic historian.

There are also about a dozen files classified as *Varia Documenta* which contain miscellaneous documents, including some of interest to the theme of the present study. These are applications submitted by individuals in need, asking economic assistance by way of alms or dowries for their daughters.[48] Although these and some other such records will have to be tapped for writing the kind of history of Goa I am advocating here, I shall introduce in more detail just one series of manuscripts entitled *Visita Pastoral.*

These manuscripts are registers of statements signed by sworn witnesses and taken down by the notary assisting the Archbishop or his delegate during the visitation of the parishes. It is customary in the Catholic Church for the Bishop to go round every few years, or as need may require, visiting every parish of his diocese to inspect the state of faith and morality of the faithful and to encourage them to do better. In Goa the non-Christians, who lived in predominantly Christian areas, were also subjected to these checks in so far as their activities could influence the Christians. The Bishop ordinarily appealed to the secular authorities to execute his sentences over non-Christians, but as to Christians he checked the record of their objectionable behaviour and determined the penalties to be executed through the parish priest, or through his own assistants if the parish priest himself was in need of correction. The abuses revealed by the sworn witnesses refer to non-observance of religious practices or lack of decorum in the practice of religion, and to such socio-economic-moral problems as drunkenness, usury, labour exploitation and prostitution.

Our records covering the years 1747-1927 are bound in 19 volumes of an average number of 300 folios. It may be noted that each of these volumes is made up of two originally separate books which still retain their original independent numbering of folios. I have culled out bits of information from the first six codices to give an idea of the source-value of these records for reconstructing the Goan past centred around village life.

(a) *Abuses in the Practice of Religion*

The parish priest of Chandor (Salcete) in 1755 is denounced by his parishioners for refusing to attend to the burial of the daughter of a widow who did not have four xerafins to pay the burial fee. The funeral was delayed until 6 p.m. when a charitable man of the village offered to pay the amount on behalf of the said widow.[49] The same priest is also accused of having refused to do the christening of the child of a poor *kunby* until he pawned his hoe to borrow half a xerafin to pay the priest.[50]

The parishioners of Siolim expressed their unhappiness over the behaviour of their assistant parish-priest in 1760. He was accused of forcibly collecting gifts from the parents of the girls who were to be approved for marriage. One of the complainants had to part with broilers worth one *xerafim*, and another had to give away a pigling costing four *xerafins*. The same priest is accused of drawing up a list of chickens and piglings the parishioners had, on the occasion of visiting their houses for the annual Easter blessings. [51]

(b) *Drunkenness*

A certain Atanasio Menezes, a married man residing in the Ganapoga ward of Rachol (Salcete) was denounced for drinking day and night. He was also accused of using his job of assistant to the police inspector of the area to pay for his drinks by extorting small cash from the poor peasants.[52]

This is one vice of which the clerics are accused with more frequency in the proceedings of the pastoral visits. Apparently, when other pleasures of the flesh were denied to them, the clerics seem to have taken the recommendation of wine by St. Paul a little too seriously. The parish-priest of Velsão (Salcete) for instance, is accused in 1748 of drinking so excessively as to be incapable of doing his duty of celebrating Mass for his parishioners even on Sundays and days of obligation. [53]

(c) *Usury*

There are plentiful references to usury in these records and this frequency perhaps rates next to prostitution.

In 1747 certain Portuguese military officials are accused of lending money to poor peasants of Jua island during the sowing season at exorbitant rates of interest. Money was lent in June to be paid back in November along with two measures of paddy per *pardau*. There were two Hindu ladies, namely Chimnea Prabu from Santa Luzia and Tuka Bamana from Kumbarjua, who were also lending money to those peasants and demanding one *kudav* of paddy per *pardau* of loan. Considering just the lesser demand of two measures, the moneylenders were collecting 148 *xerafins*, 1 *tanga* and 40 *reis* more than their due of 41-3-20 per every 1,000 *xerafins* of loan at the legitimate interest of

10% and at the market paddy price of four and half *xerafins* per fardel of 5.95 *kudav*.[54]

Cases of usury were also recorded against several men from Mormuganv (Salcete) in 1755. They were accused of lending say six *kudav* of rice in May to collect seven at the harvest time, which involved a profit of nearly 48%. Some were also lending cash in the months of January-February to be repaid in rice during the months of April-May at the rate of four to four and half *pardaus* a fardel.[55]

(d) *Exploitation of Labour*

The parish-priest of Betalbatim (Salcete) was accused in 1748 of having beaten up a *ganvkar* named André Afonso, who had refused to bring his plough to work on the parish-priest's fields, because the Fathers paid less than others for the same work.[56]

The parish-priest of Colva was accused that same year of mercilessly beating a poor man whom he had sent to Goa with a basket of mangoes and had returned without the basket and could not account for 6 mangoes which some soldiers had taken away.[57]

(e) *Prostitution*

In this matter Goa was no exception to what normally happens in places where military camps or garrisons are located. It may be noted that most of the women involved in prostitution were of low castes. Many of those found in Salcete had come from Bardez to work as cooks or house-servants. Though there were individual women offering their services freely, there were also ladies running organized brothels employing Christian and non-Christian maids.[58] One comes also across the allied problems of abortion.[59]

Church Records in the Parishes

I could not visit more than six parishes of Salcete to consult parish archives, but from this limited experience it was sufficiently clear that the keepers of those parish records were more serious in guarding the keys that kept the records safe from human visitors than in protecting them against insects and rats. With the exception of the records of the town-parish in Margão, the records in the five other village-parish were in a sad state of preservation. All that they kept in good conditions were the registers of births, marriages and deaths, which in most of the parishes date back to 1880s. The value of this sort of records cannot be minimized,[60] but there are older records going back to mid-18th century in some parishes, like Benaulim, Navelim and Margão, and which deal with the economic administration of the churches and the cult. These records of the *Fabrica* and *Confrarias* need to be salvaged with some urgency. The parish archives also have the manuscripts of the proceedings of the administrative boards of the parishes *(Junta Administrativa)* containing very useful information on the socio-economic history of the parishes. There are also the *Rois da Cristandade* giving details of age, sex and family status of the parishioners.

REFERENCES AND NOTES

1. Charles R. Boxer's authoritative and popular works, with an Eurocentric approach to the history of the Portuguese empire, may be considered responsible for the propagation of this myth in the English-speaking world. *Cf.* n. 12 *infra*. However, it also goes to the credit of Prof. Boxer to have destroyed some other myths, for which he earned the wrath of the Portuguese nationalist historians at one time. I am referring to the reactions to his *Race Relations in the Portuguese Colonial Empire 1415-1825* (Oxford, 1963). Cf. Portuguese reaction in Studia, n. 12 (July 1963), pp. 549-554. Boxer was a *persona non grata* in Portugal until the political change of 1974.
2. M. Collis, *The Land of the Great Image*, London, 1946, p. 32.
3. J.J. Gonçalves, *Síntese Bibliográfica de Goa*, 2 vols., Lisbon, 1966-7.
4. T.R. de Souza, "Hindu Enterpreneurship in Goan History", *Goa Today*, (Jan. 1978), pp. 15, 18.
5. Diogo de Couto, *O Soldado Prático*, ed. M. Rodrigues Lapa, 2nd ed., Lisbon, 1954, p. xx.
6. V. Devi, and M. Seabra, *A Literatura Indo-Portuguesa*, I, Lisbon, 1971, pp. 118-120.
7. C. M. de Melo, *The Recruitment and Formation of the Native Clergy in India*, Lisboa, 1955, p. 175.
8. For a most complete list of Cunha Rivara's works cf. N.V. Abreu, *Noção de alguns filhos distintos da India Portuguesa*, Panjim, 1874.
9. *Ibid.*
10. F.N. Xavier, *Bosquejo Historico das Communidades*, II, Panjim, 1852, p. 182.
11. P.S.S. Pissurlencar, *Agentes da Diplomacia Portuguesa na India*, Bastora, 1952.
12. Boxer, "Fidalgos Portugueses e Bailadeiras Indianas", *Revista de Historia. São Paolo*, no. 56 (1961) pp. 83-105.
13. B.G. D'Souza, *Goan Society in Transition*, Bombay, 1975.
14. A. C. Teixeira de Aragão, *Descripção Geral e Histórica das Moedas*, III, Lisbon, 1880, pp. 78-81.
15. T.R. de Souza, "Portuguese Records for Indian History at Goa and Lisbon", *The Indian Archives*, XXV, no. 1 (Jan-June 1976), pp. 24-36.
16. F. Coutinho, *Le Regime Paroissal des Dioceses de Rite Latin de l'Inde*, Louvain,

1958, p. 40.

17. *Ibid.*, p. 36.
18. Xavier, *Bosquejo Historico das Comunidades*, II, pp. 65, 71-2, 91, 107, 125.
19. *Assentos do Conselho do Estado*, ed. Pissurlencar, Bastora, 1955, III, p. 342; Bastora, 1956, IV, pp. 78 93ff., 412.
20. L. da Rocha, *As Confrarias de Goa*, Lisbon, 1973, p. 2.
21. *Documenta Indica*, ed J. Wicki (Rome, 1964): VIII, pp. 83-4; (Rome, 1972) XIII, p. 614.
22. C. M. de Melo, *op cit.*, pp. 244-251.
23. AHU: India, *Caixa* 15, doc. 110. The two priests chosen as Procurators by the general assembly were Antonio de Pinto and Estevão da Gama.
24. Bishop Matheus de Castro in the 17th century, and several priests involved in the *Conjuração dos Pintos* in the 18th century.
25. J. Wicki, *O Livro de Pai dos Cristãos*, Lisboa, 1969.
26. A. Baiäo, *Inquisição de Goa*, I, Lisbon, 1949, p. 15.
27. *Ibid.*, pp. 263-294.
28. *Ibid.*, pp. 279-283; AHU, Inddia, Caixa 41, doc. 32.
29. F. de Sousa, *Oriente Conquistado a Jesu Christo*, II, Bombay, 1886, p. 33. It was first published in Lisbon in 1710.
30. Baiäo, *op. cit.*, pp. 61, 72, 86-87, 102, 107, 123-128.
31. *Ibid.*, pp. 76-77.
32. *Cf. Supra*, no. 23.
33. HAG: Ms. 4477, fl. 16.
34. HAG: Ms. 4395, fl. 34v.
35. HAG: *Ordens Regias*, II fls. 48v-49; *ARSJ, Fondo Gesuitico:* 74-B/9, 1443; AHU, India, *Maço* 6, doc. 5 (March 11, 1755).
36. Cunha Rivara, *Archivo Portuguez-Oriental*, vol. 1, Pt. 2, p. 128.
37. HAG: *Monçöes* 19C, fl. 734v.
38. HAG: Ms. 3038, *passim*, various contracts of munda.
39. *Brotéria* (Lisbon), Photocopied documents from the Royal Archives of Belgium, Box 77, Bundle no. 1, fl. 23: contains orders fo the Provincial of the Jesuits Antonio de Almeida, in 1656 to the Brother in charge of the palm-grove, in Cortalim. He is to give alms to the poor needy mundkars.
40. HAG: Ms. 7602.
41. HAG: Ms. 860.
42. *Viagem de Francisco Pyrard de Laval*, II, ed. A. de Magalhäes Basto, Porto, 1944, p. 51.
43. *Ibid.*, p. 33.
44. HAG: Ms. 1164, *Assentos do Conselho da Fazenda*, 1643-7, fls. 164-5.
45. HAG: Mss. 2976, 2977, 3018.
46. Teixeira de Aragão, *op. cit.*, p. 80; C. de Nazareth, *Mitras Lusitanas no Oriente*, II, 2nd ed., Panjim, 1924, p. iv.
47. PA: *Offícios às Autoridades Ecclesiasticas e Civis*, 1858-62, no. 1 (1862). The folios are not numbered. It is a letter of the administrator of the archdiocese to the Archbishop-elect Amorim Pessoa requesting him to contact the brother of the former Archbishop Silva Torres and to bring back the records. Arch. Silva Torres had died in 1854 and the writer of the letter believes that his brother may be able to return the records.
48. The amount granted as alms is 5 *xerafins*. The dowry-grants vary between 25 and 30 *xerafins*.

49. PA: *Visita Pastoral*, V-VI, fl. 150v.
50. *Ibid.*
51. PA: *Visita Pastoral*, VII-VIII, fl. 86v.
52. PA: *Visita Pastoral*, III, fl. 15v.
53. *Ibid.*, fl. 55.
54. *Ibid.*, 4v-8v.
55. PA: *Visita Pastoral*, V-VI, fls. 11, 15v.
56. PA: *Visita Pastoral*, I-II, fl. 117v.
57. *Ibid.*, fls. 110v-111.
58. PA: *Visita Pastoral*, V-VI, fl. 96; IX-X, fl. 95.
59. PA: *Visita Pastoral*, V-VI, fls. 63v-64.
60. H. G. Srivastava, "Marriages among the Christians of Goa — A Study Based on Parish Registers", *The Indian Economic and Social History Review*, XIV, no. 2, pp. 247-254.

N.B. As this book goes to the press it is known that the Fundação Oriente of Portugal has provided funds for microfilming the records of the Patriarchal archives and also for the preparation of an inventory. Dr. M. Abrantes of the Portuguese Overseas Archives has been entrusted with the latter task.

[Published originally as "The Voiceless in Goan Historiography: A case for the Source-Value of Church Records in Goa", *Indo-Portuguese History: Sources and Problems*, ed. John Correia-Afonso, Bombay, Oxford University Press, 1981, pp. 114-131].

3

CHRISTIANISATION OF GOA AND CULTURAL CONFLICTS

We in India are proud of our rich historical and cultural heritage which dates far back and beyond the arrival of the Portuguese in India, and we cannot help re-assessing the impact of the Portuguese arrival and the brand of Christianity they brought to India against this background. While we admit that some of our negative cultural elements have been exposed for correction, as for instance the abolition of *sati* (the custom of widow burning) by Afonso de Albuquerque,[1] we feel culturally wounded and alienated in many respects as a result of that encounter. Surprisingly the Portuguese did nothing to end the caste system, and even ended up in reinforcing it with distinctive colours for different caste confraternities or *irmandades*.[2] We are also left wondering how the Portuguese conscience by and large could be concerned with the Hindu widows, but could see no great evil in their handling of black slavery on a mass scale, exceeding any number of widows that may have fallen victims to the Hindu culture.[3] We need to keep these paradoxes in mind while assessing the general theme of "The Portuguese missionary movement and the encounter of cultures" that is being discussed on the occasion many celebrations of 500 years of "Discoveries". More particularly, we need to pay attention to the underlying misconception about the principle of incarnation as valid only for one's own culture, and the consequent denial of transcultural faith. It may amuse today to read the account of a Jesuit writing from Goa in 1567 describing a group of newly baptised in the village Telaulim of Goa. He was tired of dressing them and cutting their *xendys* until "they looked like people in whom the Holy Spirit could dwell" (*já pareciam gente em que morava o Espirito Santo*)![4]

In this essay I wish to touch on some manifestations of popular reaction against the Portuguese missionary zeal in Goa during the 16th to 19th centuries. They may appear to be sporadic and disconnected outbursts, but they confirm an ongoing resentment that was lying low during the rest of the time for reasons not difficult to imagine. However, just as the Portuguese missionary activity cannot be explained adequately by exclusively religious motivations without other economic and political factors, so also the local native reactions were not purely religious. Religion and culture were intimately bound up with economic and political interests. It needs to be admitted that there were class differences in the Goan society and these were very well exploited by the Portuguese, just as they were exploited by the other foreign invaders of the subcontinent, like the Muslims earlier and by the British later, to "divide and rule" in the subcontinent. To quote Prof. M. G. S. Narayanan, who delivered the inaugural address at the 5th International Seminar on Indo-Portuguese History at Cochin: "The possibility of converting a socially depressed class was effectively demonstrated, and thereby the basic injustice built into the Hindu caste structure was exposed". The Vicar General Miguel Vaz, who was greatly responsible for the organised conversion drive in Goa, was writing in his memorial to the crown of Portugal in 1545: "Let us do this people favour, honour and justice, and let us not leave them at the mercy of brahmins Krishna and Gopu, about whom they have been continuously complaining. Knowing what sort of tyrants these men are, I feel that people have all the reasons to complain about them." [5] Hence, just as in the case of Islam, conversion to Christianity after the arrival of the Portuguese was seen by the marginalised social groups forming the bulk of the converts in India (with the exception of Goa where the higher castes too accepted Christianity for safeguarding their traditional privileges and status under Portuguese jurisdiction) as an opportunity for social and economic change that was denied to them within the existing traditional social structure. The failure of Christianity in India to satisfy these expectations even after several centuries has recently led to mass reconversions of Christians to Hinduism in Goa or to Islam in South India.[6]

Whatever may have been the pretensions of the Portuguese rank and file for a higher level of culture or values they intended to transmit to the lesser mortals in their *Estado da India*, we would do well to keep in mind the assessment of the Portuguese people of the period of Discoveries by Prof. Boxer in the Prologue to his *The Portuguese Seaborne Empire*: "Medieval Europe was a harsh and rugged school, and the softer graces of civilisation were not more widely cultivated in

Portugal than they were elsewhere. A turbulent and treacherous nobility and gentry; an ignorant and lax clergy; doltish if hard-working peasants and fishermen; and an urban rabble of artisans and day-labourers like the Lisbon mob described by the greatest of the Portuguese novelists, Eça de Queiroz later, as 'fanatical, filthy and ferocious' (*essa plebe beata, suja, e feroz*); these constituted the social classes from which the pioneer discoverers and colonisers were drawn".[7] Vasco da Gama has been described as a rough and even brutal nature who certainly had little interest in India except the commercial one, and but for the anecdote that he and his followers worshipped in a Hindu temple mistaking a Hindu goddess for Virgin Mary, they left no information about Hindu religion or society.[8] This assessment is amply supported and documented by Prof. G.D. Winius in *The Black Legend of Portuguese India* (New Delhi, Concept Publ. Co., 1985), wherein he draws from contemporary sources a picture of the *Estado da India* which survived not so much on trade, as on institutionalised corruption. This is confirmed by St. Francis Xavier when writing to Fr. Simão Rodrigues in Portugal: "Allow no friends of yours to come to India with offices and nominations from the king, because of these people one can truly say: 'Let them be blotted out of the book of the living, and not be written with the righteous'."[9]

The missionaries that came to the East were certainly the more educated lot of the European society, but they were no less a product of the same mentality. The Jesuit annual reports and other contemporary missionary writings refer frequently to "devil at work" while referring to any opposition to the missionary activity or to continued practice of non-Christian religions. It implies a mentality that was closed to seeing God at work in traditional native religions and their cultures. We in India today cannot accept such a facile and simplistic categorisation of resistance to the missionary activities or give them the credit of martyrdom. The incidents need to be further analysed in the local context to understand better the cultural conflicts that the natives had to undergo in the process of Christianisation at the hands of the European missionaries. There was no mental disposition on the part of most foreign missionaries to see anything good in the native cultures. The Italian missionaries, as a result of their political-cultural background of commercial city-states in Europe were perhaps better disposed than the other European missionaries coming from nation-states to appreciate native cultures. But even then it was more of a strategic accomodation, rather than a sincere appreciation of native cultures. The Portuguese João de Brito was an exception, but even in his case we know nothing of his contribution to the local culture as in the case of De Nobili or Beschi. The most noteworthy contribution to Konkani language in Goa was made by an English Jesuit.[10]

Politico-Economic Compulsions and Missionary Zeal

The Portuguese rule had begun in Goa by wooing the local Hindu leadership to drive its Muslim rulers out. Afonso de Albuquerque had made public promises to respect the native customs based on *Dharmashastras*, which were Hindu religious law books. However, as soon as the Portuguese felt they were firmly in control of Goa they saw no further need to stand by those promises.[11] As the overseas empire of the Portuguese with its headquarters in Goa began eating itself as a result of growing bureaucracy, religious groups and their dependents, and dwindling external resources, the counter-Reformation zeal became an effective tool to legitimise the process of absorbing the local resources of Goa.[12] With their capacity to terrorise the native populations into submission, not unlike the Muslims earlier, the Portuguese had displayed an effective combination of military force and missionary zeal, of gunboats accompanied by military chaplains.[13] Even a letter of St. Francis Xavier to Ignatius of Loyola suggests that the Christianity in India will survive and prosper only in the coastal regions within the reach of Portuguese gunboats.[14]

The see of the new diocese of Goa was not occupied till 1538 by the Franciscan recollect Juan de Albuquerque. The establishment of a confraternity of Holy Faith and the arrival of Jesuit militancy in Goa initiated an organised conversion drive which the natives were in no position to withstand. Many natives left Goa or were forced to leave it, while others accepted Christianity either willingly for overcoming the traditional social and economic disabilities, or under pressure of legislation that was enacted by the Portuguese making the public practice of Hindu cult and inherited cultural practices difficult. The traditional native life-style was being subverted by Portuguese legislation designed to favour promotion of Christianity.[15] Hence, it is true what the Jesuit historians like S.G. Perera or Henry Heras stated about the Portuguese not using sword to convert Asians to Christians.[16] But it is untrue that no violence was used. It would be an acceptable definition of violence only against animals, but not valid for human persons, if violence is defined only in terms of crude physical violence without accepting economic, social, and psychological pressures as effective means of doing violence.[17]

XVI Century: Cuncolim Martyrs or Europe's Martyrs?

There was little violent defiance of the Portuguese policy of demolishing Hindu temples and various anti-Hindu laws in the islands of Goa, but the natives of more distant and frontier village of Cuncolim in Salcete (south Goa) expressed their resentment violently by killing five Jesuits and some others who accompanied them with the intention of implanting the new religion there in 1583. As a result of its location on the upper course of Sal river and consequent availability of abundant waters for irrigation Cuncolim had a good agricultural base. Its surplus agricultural produce, plus its location at the cross-roads of three Ghat-passages had enabled also development of skilled handicrafts and commerce in this village. Cuncolim was specially noted for its metalworks, including gun-manufacturing. The main temple of Mahadeva in Cuncolim was near its market-place (*bazar*) and the fairs on the occasion of religious festivals were very important for the economic life of the village and for the social classes benefiting from it. It is against this background that one needs to examine the reaction of the natives to the destruction of the temple and the killing of the Jesuits who sought to replace the traditional faith with Christianity.[18]

If we are to believe that the introduction of Christianity would make a difference to the village, it was sad to observe large-scale disturbance in Cuncolim in 1983 (fourth centenary of the "martyrdom") when the dominant caste families decided to take over the control of the parish church, declare it "independent Church of Cuncolim", and place an idol of goddess Mhamai on the main altar. A priest of the same caste and supporting the cause took charge of the Church. The archbishop could reassert his authority and regain control of the premises only through the court of justice and the assistance of police. The social divisions have not healed and the tensions are dormant since then.

We have a long account of the case sent to Rome by the Jesuit visitor at the time, Fr. Valignano.[19] The names of two native boys who were accompanying the priests and were killed along with the Jesuits are mentioned, but they have never figured in the Church list of the *beati* of Cuncolim! The Polish Mgr. Ladislas Michel Zaleski, the Apostolic Delegate who set up the Indian hierarchy in 1886 and author of *The Saints of India* (1915) has a very pertinent remark: "Why should the secular priests of India recite the office of Saints of foreign countries, who have for them no special interest, and neglect and ignore the particular Saints of India, their Patrons and Protectors?" He follows the argument in the Chapter dealing with Bl. Rudolf Acquaviva and companions: "It should be examined if these Indian Martyrs (...) could not be included in the beatification. The two last named (young Dominic and Alphonso) (...) would be wonderful patrons for Indian youths and boys".[20] This reminds me of a bold comment of the eminent Portuguese historian of discoveries Jaime Cortesão: "A national religion creates its own saints and its advocates in the heavenly court"! [21] The white Jesuit martyrs and beati served the cause of the Portuguese military-religious complex in Goa. Rougher measures were adopted to put an end to Hindu cult and culture in Salcete, local village communities were abolished in Cuncolim and its four satellite villages, the whole of Salcete was brought under complete Portuguese administrative control and the Hindu temple properties were handed over to the Jesuits. It was the foundation of the wealth of the Jesuits in Goa and it it was greatly responsible for their doom under the regime of Pombal.[22]

XVII Century: D. Matheus de Castro Mahale

This first Goan Brahmin consecrated Bishop and sent as a Vicar Apostolic to the Grand Mughal by the Propaganda Fide in the mid-seventeenth century represents another example of the native reaction to the "encounter" in the sense of confrontation, rather than a friendly meeting of cultures that resulted from the Portuguese-sponsored Christianisation of Goa.

The Jesuit strategy in the conversion movement had been to win over the higher castes in an effort to draw over the rest of the populace. It worked to some extent, till the Brahmin priests of the secular clergy realised the injustices they were victims of. In a 9-point memorandum to Rome they accused the Jesuits of persecuting them and had been sending false information against them and the Bishop Matheus de Castro who had to flee to Rome as a result.[23] This native bishop was not allowed to function in the Portuguese territory, and he avenged himself by inciting both the Muslim Sultan of Bijapur and the Calvinist Dutch East India Company to attack Goa.[24] The Portuguese repaid his dislike with interest, the venerable Jesuit Patriarch of Ethiopia, the Jesuit Dom Alfonso Mendes, terming the Brahmin bishop "a bare-bottomed nigger".[25]

The foreign Religious Orders in Goa patronised the natives to the extent they were required to fulfil unavoidable subsidiary roles. The Jesuits used the Brahmins and later the Chardos, following the lead of Francis Xavier, to function as interpreters in their parishes and missions.

Yet when these natives were proving troublesome, lower castes seem to have been inducted into the priesthood to offset the increasing hostility of the higher caste clerics like D. Matheus de Castro.[26] Many of the natives who became priests were soon disillusioned: Their hopes of being treated as equals along with the Religious remained a dream. The religious clergy kept them lower on various grounds in order to guarantee for themselves higher positions and to maintain their own authority.[27]

XVIII Century: The Pinto Conspiracy

This is yet another case of frustrated reaction of Goan native priests and laymen who saw no hopes of promotions based on merit for the natives in a Portuguese colonial set-up. The conspiracy to overthrow the Portuguese rule in Goa was discovered and suppressed ruthlessly by the Portuguese administration after a summary trial based on extraction of evidence from the accused under torture. As a result fourteen priests remained under house arrest in Portuguese monasteries without trial for eighteen years before being granted pardon, fifteen native military men were hanged, and further ten civilians were deported or condemned to serve in galleys. The conspiracy was masterminded by two priests, namely Caetano Francisco do Couto and Jose Antonio Gonçalves, both of whom had been in Portugal to claim appointments for the vacant sees of Cranganore and Mylapore. A foreign hand was suspected, because Goa was living under the threat of an invasion by Tipu Sultan of Mysore. The Bhosle of Sawant Wadi was also mounting repeated attacks on Goa. At the end of the trial it was found that no foreign power was involved, but there was still the feeling that if the hostile neighbours had found out about the rebellion they would not hesitate to exploit the situation to their advantage. The trial results were kept secret, but it confirmed the conviction that it was a social political and racial uprising. In spite of Pombal's decree of April 2, 1761 commanding that Asiatic subjects of the Portuguese crown should have the same rights as the metropolitan Portuguese, the situation in India did not improve. Almost all the correspondence intercepted and used for the trial emphasized the feeling of social and racial discrimination felt by the Goans. The clergy and the military were the main professions to feel the brunt of such discrimination. The influence of American Independence was evident, but there is no clarity about the form of government the rebels had in mind, though some ideas of Fr. Gonçalves on this matter were voiced by some of the witnesses and these definitely did not imply any equality of rights for all Goans. There had been a similar rebellion around the same time in Brazil, and these incidents revealed the same malaise that was current in the Portuguese colonial world.[28]

While the above two cases reveal more violent tendencies and reactions of cultural conflict in Portuguese Goa, the seventeenth and eighteen centuries also saw the establishment and progress of the Congregation of the Oratory in Goa by some native priests as an alternative to their exclusion from dignified membership in the Religious Orders which were still a foreign preserve. Fr. Joseph Vaz and his companions in this Congregation did an excellent job in safeguarding the Catholic Church in Sri Lanka to which the Portuguese missionaries had no access after its capture by the Dutch. Goan Oratorians will be forever remembered as the "Aspostles of Ceylon". It was a successful model of Christianisation that was not based on a large-scale organisation or depend on political-military support of the European colonial type.[29]

XIX Century: Padre Alvares (Mar Julius I)

In the last quarter of the nineteenth century it was Fr. Antonio Francisco Xavier Alvares from Verna (Salcete) who embodied the frustrations of the Goans. He was an editor, writer, and founder of educational welfare institutions. He left the Church in which he was ordained to join the Syrian Orthodox Church which consecrated him bishop of Goa, India and Ceylon with the title of Mar Julius I. In his book entitled *A Supremacia Universal da Igreja de Cristo* (Colombo, 1889), Fr. Alvares has a tirade against the abuses of the Padroado and he denounced the unholy alliance of the Papacy with temporal rulers to enhance its authority. He was conscious that it was in Asia that God's revelation had taken place first, and he blamed the Europeans for distorting it. Through his newspaper *O Brado Indiano* he conducted a determined campaign against the Portuguese administrative and ecclesiastical abuses.[30] Not surprisingly he invited the wrath of both ecclesiastical and civil authorities who excomunicated him and charged him with sedition. He was stripped of his episcopal garments and paraded only with his underwear in a horse-driven car through the streets of Panjim by a Portuguese army officer, Capt. Gomes da Costa, who had a grudge against him.

When he died, his body was carried in a huge funeral procession, in which thousands of natives participated, to Santa Ines cemetery, after his body lay in state for a full day dressed in a bishop's full regalia, complete with the mitre and the crozier. There were four funeral orations!

Fr. Alvares had spent some years in Bombay and English education had given his mind a more secular exposure away from the narrow Church-influenced mentality of the Goan society. On return to Goa he exercised his priesthood as an apostle of the poor, sick and the marginalised, both physically and through his writings, drawing attention and anger of irresponsible and arrogant authorities in the Church and the Government who were at this time also neurotic about *nativist revolt* following a Maratha sepoy revolt and the Dada Rane revolt.[31] Fr. Alvares was declared to be a threat to the security of the State and a rebel against the religion of the Kingdom (Portugal). None of these charges could be substantiated in the court of law, and the Military Police Chief then decided to put chains on him on an unbailable charge of high treason. Even then the courts exonerated him.[32]

He had crossed 80 when he died as a poor man, collecting alms and begging from door to door with a trembling hand to support himself and the other poor and neglected sick people he had taken under his care. The holiness of the man is revealed by an incident when an enraged shop-keeper instead of dropping a coin in Fr. Alvares' bowl, spat in it. Without getting annoyed, the priest gently replied: "All right, I shall keep this for me. Now, give something for my poor". The shop-keeper could not but apologise and contribute more generously.[33]

Concluding Remarks

The above selection of cases should suffice to bring out the nature of dissatisfaction that rankled in the hearts of many prominent native Goan leaders who were in a position to understand and analyse the impact of the Portuguese rule and their missionary activity in Goa. There is no denying the fact that it exposed some of the internal contradictions and injustices embedded in the native culture and social structures, but it also destroyed much of the ancient Goan temple art, literature, and communal harmony. Referring to the destruction of the temples and idols in Salcete, an early Jesuit report says: "Some were burnt down, others were heaped as garbage, and still others were razed to the ground. Nearly 280 of these were big ones and some of them very sumptuous and of exceedingly fine workmanship."[34] It was not just the architecture of the temples that mattered, the temples in the ancient Hindu culture were also the repositories of literature that was mainly of religious nature and were centres of learning and teaching. The Portuguese missionaries introduced the first printing press in Goa, but they also sought to destroy the existing books on Hinduism in Goa.[35]

Perhaps on the positive side the Portuguese missionaries and colonial government prepared the Goans to adjust early and better to the values and culture of a world capitalist order of the West, while being alienated from their native cultural roots. It has been a very mixed legacy of few gains and many losses; more so for those who have to live and build the future of Goans in Goa alongside and in competition with Goa's 65% Hindu majority that has not forgotten the discrimination and disabilities they suffered under the Portuguese rule and as a result of their holding on to their Hindu past.

REREFERENCES AND NOTES

1. J.A. Ismael Gracias, "Albuquerque e as mulheres Indianas", *O Oriente Portugues*, n. 1 & 2, 1916, pp. 1-10.
2. Leopoldo da Rocha, *As Confrarias de Goa*, Lisboa, 1973, pp. 284 ff.
3. C. R. Boxer, "As raizes de Portugal em Africa, 1415-1800", *Balanço da Colonizaçao Portuguesa*, Lisboa, Iniciativas, 1975, pp. 111-131; C.R. Boxer, *Race Relations in the Portuguese Colonial Empire*, 1415-1825, Connecticut: Grenwood Press, 1985; *Navio Negreiro*, ed. CEHILA, São Paulo, Edições Paulinas, 1981; José Capela e Eduardo Medeiros, *O trafico de escravos de Moçambique para as ilhas do Indico*, Universidade Eduardo Mondlane, 1987; B.H. Baden-Powell, "The Villages of Goa in the Early Sixteenth Century", The *Journal of the Royal Asiatic Society*, London, 1900, pp. 261-291.0
4. *Documenta Indica*, VII, ed. J. Wicki, Rome, 1962, p. 301.
5. *Documenta Indica*, I, ed. J. Wicki, Rome, 1948, pp. 68, 70.
6. Archana Kakodkar, "Shuddhi: Reconversion to Hinduism movement in Goa", *Goa: Cultural Trends*, ed. P.P. Shirodkar, Panaji, 1988, pp. 242-263; Mumtaz Ali Khan, "Mass conversions of Meenakshipuram: A sociological inquiry", *Religion in South Asia*, ed. G.A. Oddie, Delhi, Manohar Publications, 1991, pp. 47-63; Duncan B. Forrester, "The depressed classes and conversion to Christianity, 1860-1960", *ibid.*, pp. 65-93.
7. C. R. Boxer, *The Portuguese Seaborne Empire, 1415-1825*, London, Hutchinson & Co., 1977, pp. 3-4.
8. Jarl Charpentier, *The Livro da Seita dos Indios Orientais of Father Jacobo Fenicio, S.J.*, Upsala, 1933, pp. x-lxxxv contain an excellent introduction about the knowledge of Hinduism in the West. Considers the contribution of Jesuits as very important in this respect, but they were mostly non-Portuguese Jesuits who stand out.
9. *Epistolae S. Francisci Xaverii aliaque eius scripta*, I, ed. G. Schurhammer & J. Wicki, Rome, 1944, pp. 281-282.
10. Anand Amaladass, "Jesuits and Sanskrit Studies", *Jesuits in India: In Historical Perspective*, ed. Teotonio R. de Souza & Charles J. Borges, Macau, 1992, pp.

210-236; Matthew Almeida, "Jesuit Contribution to Indian Languages", *ibid.*, pp. 196-208.

11. Teotonio R. de Souza, *Medieval Goa*, New Delhi, Concept Publ., 1979, pp. 69-72.
12. Goa was conquered in 1510 from Adilshah of Bijapur. The headquarters were shifted from Cochin to here twenty years later. Goa then became one of the largest commercial cities in the East, and as a result the pressures on the native land and services began to increase.
13. M.N. Pearson, *Coastal Western India*, New Delhi, Concept Publ., 1981, pp. 18-40. Incidentally, it is also interesting to note the popularity of devotion to St. Sebastian in the Portuguese *Estado da India*. This was a soldier-martyr of the Roman empire, and apparently the devotion was carried by the Portuguese military for motivating the Portuguese servicemen to die for the empire convinced that they were dying for faith as well.
14. *Epistolae S. Francisci Xaverii*, II, Rome, 1945, pp. 9-10. To this suggestion one modern and outstanding Jesuit theologian of India reacted saying that in such a case the Portuguese Christianity ought not have survived!
15. *O Livro do Pai dos Cristãos*, ed. J. Wicki, Lisboa, 1969.
16. S.G. Perera, *Portuguese Missionary Methods or the Myth of "Forced Conversions"*, Colombo, 1936; H. Heras, *The Conversion Policy of the Jesuits in India*, Bombay, 1933.
17. C. R. Boxer, "A Note on Portuguese Missionary Methods in the East, 16th - 18th Centuries", *Ceylon Historical Journal*, X, nos. 1-4 (July 1960-April 1961), pp. 77-90. Boxer refutes Fr. Perera's unqualified statement, and that could be applicable also to Fr. Heras' apologetic discourse.
18. Teotonio R. de Souza, "Why Cuncolim Martyrs? An Historical Re-assessment", *Jesuits in India: In Historical Perspective*, pp. 36-47.
19. *Documenta Indica*, XII, ed. J. Wicki, Rome, 1972, pp. 916-932.
20. Ladislas-Michel Zaleski, *The Saints of India*, Mangalore, 1915, pp. 7-9.
21. Jaime Cortesão, *Os Descobrimentos Portugueses*, II, Lisboa, Livros Horizonte, 1975, p. 384.
22. *Documenta Indica*, VII, pp. 392-4; IX, pp. 336-42.
23. Jesuit Curia Archives (Rome): *Fondo Gesuitico* 1443/9; *Goa* 22, I, fls. 59-65. A tract written by a Jesuit to disprove the accusations. *Cf.* C.J. Borges, "Racial Tensions of the Society of Jesus before 1759", *Jesuits in India: In Historical Perspective*, pp. 62-71; "Foreign Jesuits and Native Resistance in Goa", *Essays in Goan History*, ed. Teotonio R. de Souza, New Delhi, Concept Publ., 1989, pp. 69-80. Charles J. Borges, *Economics of Goa Jesuits: An explanation of their rise and fall, 1542-1759* (Unpublished Ph.D. dissertation, Bombay University, 1989. Due to appear shortly in print).
24. T. R. de Souza, "An Unsung Hero: Matheus de Castro Mahale", *Goa Today*, Panjim, January 1975, pp. 18, 28. The Jesuit Gonçalo Martins was sent as a special envoy of the Goa Government to the Sultan of Bijapur in 1654 to work out the peace terms. *Cf.* "Gonçalo Martins: A Jesuit Procurator, Businessman and Diplomat in the *Estado da India*", *mare Liberum*, Lisbon, n. 5, July 1993, pp. 119-128.
25. C. R. Boxer, *Race Relations in the Portuguese Colonial Empire*, pp. 67-68.
26. A. Baião, *A Inquisição de Goa*, I, Lisboa, 1949, pp. 285-6. Refers to 3 Goan *shudra* priests formed by the Jesuits and hauled before the Inquisition in 1736.
27. C. R. Boxer, *The Church Militant and Iberian Expansion, 1440-1770*, Balti-

more, The John Hopkins University Press, 1978, pp. 95-96.

28. J. H. da Cunha Rivara, *A Conjuração de 1787 em Goa*, Nova Goa, 1875 (Reprinted by Asian Educations Services, New Delhi, 1990). This view and more recent views of outside involvement in the conspiracy have been refuted by Ernestina Carreira with the help of more material from the archives of Lisbon and France. Cf. Ernestina Carreira, "Goa in the Reign of Tipoo Sultan: International politics and the Pinto's conspiracy" (Unpublished paper presented at the Fifth International Seminar on Indo-Portuguese History, Cochin, January 1989).
29. C. R. Boxer, *Race Relations*, p. 68; Teotonio R. de Souza, "Oratorians in Goa (1682-1835)", *Goa: Cultural Trends*, ed. P.P Shirodkar, Panaji, 1988, pp. 141-150.
30. Pratima Kamat, "Some Protesting Priests of Goa", *Essays in Goan History*, p. 114.
31. Carmo Azevedo, *Patriot and Saint: The Life Story of Father Alvares / Bishop Mar Julius I*, Panjim, 1988. For more details about the political situation at this time, *Cf.* Roberto Bruto da Costa, *A Hidra do Nativismo*, Nova Goa, 1920; Visconde de Bardez (Inacio Caetano de Carvalho), *Apontamentos para a História da Revolta dos Soldados, Ranes e Satarienses (1895)*, Bombaim, 1896; Gomes da Costa, *A revolta de Goa e a Campanha de 1895/1896*, Lisboa, 1939.
32. Carmo Azevedo, *Ibid.*, p. 30.
33. *Ibid.*, p. 44.
34. *Documenta Indica*, VII, p. 391.
35. *Documenta Indica*, IV, pp. 309 ff., 335, 669 ff. Incidentally it is suprising that Akbar showed no great interest in the printing press introduced by the Jesuits. Apparently he found it to be too crude in comparison with the calligraphic art work that he knew of.

[This is a revised version of "Christianization and cultural conflict in Goa: 16th to 19th centuries", Proceedings of the internacional congress on *Missionação portuguesa e encontro de culturas*, Braga, 1992, vol.IV, pp. 383-393.]

4

THE ORATORIANS OF GOA (1682-1835)
A Model of Non-colonial Missionary Approach

The Oratorians of Goa have carved out for themselves a lasting memorial in the living church of Sri Lanka and will be forever remembered as "the Apostles of Ceylon". It was achieved without fanfare, with a small and fragile organization, and surely with no backing of gunboats. It was an achievement of a band of Goan natives, who were regarded as unfit for religious life, and much less for missionary work, in a colonial ecclesiastical set-up marked by white superiority.

In December 1984, I was given an opportunity by the authorities of the Goa Archdiocese to deliver two public lectures on the occasion of the exposition of the relics of St. Francis Xavier. In one of these lectures, I compared the missionary methods of the Apostle of the Indies and of the Apostle of Ceylon, and I presented them as incomparable in their own fields. One could not replace the other.[1]

It is felt that the Oratorians of Goa, rightfully deserve a place in any comprehensive cultural history of Goa. It would not be out of place to recall the tribute paid to them by our veteran historian of the Portuguese empire, Prof. C.R. Boxer: "More effective than the intrigues of this stormy petrel, (referring to the Brahmin Bishop Matheus de Castro) in breaking down the doctrine of white superiority in church and state, was the apostolic action of a group of Goan Oratorians headed by Fr. Joseph Vaz".[2]

It is not possible here in this brief paper to define all the basic canonical-juridical concepts that distinguish a Religious Order from a Religious Congregation, or a public oratory from a semi-public oratory and private oratory, or simple religious vows from the solemn profession. By at least mentioning these distinctions, I wish to sound a note of caution and invite the students of Church history or an allied subject to take the trouble to grasp all the required doctrinal-juridical finer points underlying the various historical developments in the church. One notices too often the shallowness of historians in our country on this count.

An attempt is made here to bring to the notice of some readers some new information resources, or at least raise some fresh questions. In fact, I have very little to add to the unbeatable scholarship of Fr. S. G. Perera, S.J.[3] and to the overwhelming output of Fr. V. Perniola, S.J.[4] Between the two of them they have reduced greatly the margin of new secrets about the Oratorians of Goa from turning up in the various archives! Anyone researching on the Oratorians of Goa would be happy to know that Ms. 7536 entitled "*Despeza do Colégio de S. Tomas*" in the series of *Papéis dos Conventos Extintos* of the Historical Archives of Goa (HAG) is actually a sacristy-book of the Casa de S. Cruz dos Milagres containing important obituaries of the Oratorians for the years 1819-34.

Before proceeding with the summary account of the origin, activities and suppression of the Oratorians of Goa, it is better to turn to the major archival and bibliographical sources that cover this theme and need to be consulted for any serious study of the Oratorians of Goa. Whatever its shortcomings and panegyric excesses, the *Vida do Venerável Padre José Vaz* by one-time Oratorian, Fr. Sebastião do Rego, remains a classic reading on the subject.[5] The bibliography of S.G. Perera marks a pioneering phase that provided archival base to the study of the Oratorians of Goa. Perera's biographies of Joseph Vaz and Jacome Gonçalves will remain standard works on these missionaries and their congregation. Perera was well-prepared for his task after completing his scholarly translation of Fr. Fernão Queiroz's monumental work, *The Temporal and Spiritual Conquest of Ceylon* (3 vols. Colombo, 1930). While Perera published the English translations of select documents (55 docs.) from the archives of Lisbon and Goa in a series of 50 page-booklets each (6 in all, 1636-1638), he made the Portuguese texts available to Nicolau João J. de Menezes, who published them serially in *O Oriente Portugues* (Bastora, *New Series* 1937-1939) under the title "*Os Milagristas: Subsídios para a sua história*".

Another important contribution to the study of the Oratorians of Goa was made by M. da Costa Nunes, who had served in the Goa Archdiocese for four years and was later appointed Rector of the *Instituto Portugues de Santo António* in Rome. His *Documentação para a História da Congregação do Oratório de Santa Cruz dos Milagres do Clero Natural de Goa* (Lisboa: CEHU, 1966) contains texts of 144 documents on the Oratorians of Goa extracted from the various archives of Lisbon and Évora. He has also reprinted some documents already published by J. H. da Cunha Rivara in his *Archivo Portuguez-Oriental* and *O Chronista do Tissuary*. This precious and bulky volume of 775 pages was produced to promote the cause of beatification of Fr. Joseph Vaz, and also to counter the critics of the Portuguese "racist" attitude towards the native clergy.[6]

Some documents, or to be precise, ten letters of Fr. Joseph Vaz were published in 1957 by R. Boudens, O.M.I., in his book *The Catholic Church in Ceylon under Dutch Rule* (Rome, 1957). It was from 1976 that the former Jesuit Provincial Superior of Sri Lanka, Fr. V. Perniola, undertook to complete the work of S.G. Perera and make available in one series of volumes a full translation of the Oratorian documents. The first three volumes covering 1658-1795 and entitled *The Catholic Church in Sri Lanka* are already available in print with 421 documents altogether, plus valuable introductions and annotations. Most of the relevant documents from the HAG relating to the Oratorians of Goa have appeared or will appear in *The Catholic Church in Sri Lanka*. While saying "most of the relevant material", it is important to qualify it, and there is seen the scope for further research to be done by us. More work needs to be done upon the background of those who joined the Oratory, and more light needs to be shed upon the life and activities of the Oratorians in Goa, particularly upon their handling of the academic responsibilities entrusted to them in the seminaries of Chorão and Rachol in the wake of the suppression of the Society of Jesus.

It is said that they were quite popular as preachers in the villages of Goa and there is one curious case of their being called upon by the Archbishop D. Fr. Agostinho da Annunciação to assist in the village of Anjuna, which had been struck by a small-pox epidemic. Four Oratorians were sent post-haste in obedience to the order. This was in February 1705.[7] More such details and more light on the Goan angle of the Oratorian story will help us enrich our cultural history.

The Oratorians in Goa were not living just trusting upon the Providence and without worrying about the means of their sustenance and support of their missionary activity. Their correspondence with the Viceroys and with Lisbon is constantly reminding the State authorities to raise their allowances. HAG has records of the properties and donations (*pensões*) made in perpetuity in favour of the Oratorians by their many well-wishers. From the details published by J.B. Amancio Gracias in *O Oriente Português* (1937) one can begin to understand the accusations that were directed against the Oratorians by non-natives.[8] However, so far no documentary evidence is traced which would support the opinion that the Oratorians were lavish in their use of available funds. If there are any stray cases of abuses in this respect, that happened in Sri Lanka after the Oratorians had entered in a phase of amicable relations with the Dutch in the last quarter of the 18th century.[9]

Now, it is worth tracing the story of what brought the Oratorians of Goa into existence, the opposition they faced in this process, and their remarkable successes till their suppression in 1835. To cut a long story short, the majority of European-born Portuguese were convinced up-holders of white superiority. This is clear from the history of the Religious Orders and of the armed forces of Portuguese India. After some preliminary hesitation, and the admission of a few Indians or half-castes to their ranks, all the Religious Orders refused to admit these categories by the end of the 16th century, and they maintained this policy for over a century, and the Jesuits particularly did not open their ranks to the natives of India till their suppression and restoration.

For more background and prejudices and colonial interests involved in this issue one should refer to *Race Relations in the Portuguese Colonial Empire* (1963) and *The Church Militant and Iberian Expansion* (1978) of Prof. Boxer, and to *The Recruitment and Formation of the Native Clergy in India* (1955) by Carlos Merces de Melo, S.J. There was never any problem about the natives being ordained secular priests, but they were kept in a subordinate positions and functioned as glorified catechists in most cases. But since 1622 and the foundation of the Sacred Congregation for the Propagation of Faith (known in brief as *Propaganda Fide* or simply *Propaganda*) the momentum was building up for offering greater responsibilities to the native clergy in their home countries. That is how Matheus de Castro, Custódio Pinho and Tomas de Castro were consecated Bishops in *partibus infidelium* and sent as Vicars Apostolic to the territories outside Portuguese effective political control in India. But within Goa the *Padroado* Church resisted such moves even after Pombal's orders to the contrary and till the suppression of all Religious Orders in 1833-35 left no other option but to raise the status of the secular clergy, including their native counterparts in the colonies.[10]

It was against this background that when a holy and aged priest, Pascoal da Costa Jeremias, felt called to a life of religious perfection, he had no help but to strike out a path for himself. Her persuaded four other like-minded to join him in an attempt to lead a religious life in community. In 1682 they began the experiment with a brief and elementary Rule of Life approved by the Archbishop of Goa. They went into residence in the chapel of St. John of the Desert at Batim. Unfortunately, the dilapidated building standing on a lone and unhealthy hill-top proved most unsuitable, and Fr. Pascoal's four companions decided to leave him alone with St. John in the Desert! But their desertion was made up by two more intrepid souls that came to share the hope and desolation of Fr. Pascoal. Trials continued: In the rainy season of 1683 the chapel collapsed, and the problems caused by the invasion of Sambhaji removed all hope of rebuilding it. The three spiritual adventurers migrated to Goa and were given the abandoned church of the Holy Cross of Miracles for their abode. [11]

Here the small community seemed to stagnate and was threatening to dissolve when on 25th September, 1685, a young and zealous priest, Fr. Joseph Vaz of Sancoale sought to join the band. He had been moved by the harrowing tales of the plight of the Catholics of Ceylon under the Dutch rule. His request to go there had been changed by the Church authorities of Goa to an appointment for Kanara as Vicar Forane. Kanara had also come under the Dutch control at this time, and the Church of Goa did not look with favour the presence of D. Custodio de Pinho as Vicar Apostolic sent by the *Propaganda Fide* to that area. Father Vaz was thus being used to maintain a semblance of the *Padroado* jurisdiction in Kanara, but he handled his appointment deftly for three years (1681-84) without getting himself drawn into the *Padroado-Propaganda* conflict.[12] He had also used his acquaintance with the situation in Kanara to study the ways of entering Ceylon unnoticed, preferably as a slave of the Dutch Company whose ships called at the ports of Kanara for trade. When the Archbishop D. Antonio Brandão died in January 1684, Fr. Vaz seized the opportunity to return to Goa. Here he was received coldly for not having asserted himself against the Vicar Apostolic, and was not given charge of any benefice. That is when he saw a more effective way of realising his desire of serving the Church in Sri Lanka, namely of joining the newly formed Congregation of native priests and thereby ensuring the continuity of his efforts and the required organizational backing.[13]

Fr. Joseph Vaz was heartily welcomed and was forthwith chosen Superior of the yet nameless community. The first thing the new Superior did was to decide what they wanted to be, and they finally decided to adopt the rules and statutes of some existing Congregation, and that turned out to be the Oratory of St. Philip Neri. The Oratories of St. Philip are congregations of secular priests living under obedience but without vows. Their aim is prayer, preaching and the administration of the sacraments. Fr. Vaz and companions wrote to the founder of the Oratory in Lisbon, Fr. Bartolomeo de Quental, who replied to them most favourably. In the meantime, Fr. Vaz departed with two companions in the direction of Sri Lanka with the secrecy that was required. The companions deserted him in Tellicherry when they got to know the real destination! This would be quoted later against the group as a sign of inconsistency, raising doubts about their fitness for being approved as a Religious Congregation.[14]

The canonical institution of the Oratory proved to be a hard task. Dom Pedro da Silva, Bishop of Cochin and *sede vacante* Administrator of Goa Archdiocese was positively against the idea of an Oratory in Goa. What he did not like above all was the exemption from episcopal control that the Oratories enjoyed. There was also the bad impression created that the *Milagristas*, as the community was generally called, suffered from instability as manifested by the first four companions of Father Pascoal and the desertion of Fr. Vaz by his two companions. Another objection, and a more serious one, not generally mentioned in the official sources but found in an anonymous manuscript,[15] was that the Oratory was intended only for Brahmins. But though the *Milagristas* replied that it was open to all and actually received some members of the other castes, the Oratory consisted mostly of Brahmins. This could explain also why in late 18th century the Third Order of Carmelites established in a convent at Chimbel became a ghetto of the native priests of the rival *chardo* caste.[16] This interesting cultural phenomenon needs to be noted. The intercaste rivalry and conflicts among the Christian natives constitute an important feature of our cultural past and also present!

To return to the story, when a new Archbishop, D. Fr. Agostinho de Anunciação arrived, he too was opposed to the idea of an Oratory. But in the meantime the great work that Fr. Vaz was doing in Sri Lanka was becoming known and admired. Fr. Vaz had also been sending urgent appeals for more men from his community. The prelate in the meantime remained adamant in his resistance to their formal recognition unless their constitution left their supreme direction in his own hands. The Oratorians of Lisbon and Rome came to their rescue with strong appeals to the Holy See. The Roman authorities did not seem to favour the requirements of the Archbishop and wished the Oratory to be such as St.

Philip Neri had instituted it. In 1706 Clement XI issued a Bull approving the establishment of an Oratory in Goa. The Archbishop wished to suspend the execution of the Bull on the grounds that it went counter to the royal decree wnich subjected the Oratory to the Archbishop's control. But at the instance of the Viceroy, he refrained from doing so, on condition that the members of the Congregation accepted his direction. But then again the Oratory of Lisbon approached the King and obtained the acceptance of the Papal Bull. Thus, on 30 March, 1709 the Oratory of the Holy Cross of Miracles received Papal and Royal approbation and was duly established in Goa. [17]

When the Oratory was thus established, novices began to come in and the Congregation felt the need of a larger convent. They asked for and obtained the Carmelite convent that had been practically unused since the expulsion of the Italian Carmelites from the Portuguese territory in 1702. The island of Sri Lanka became the distinctive field of missionary activity of the Oratory. From time to time the Oratory also sent missionaries to Malabar, Madagascar, Solor and Timor. On the suppression of the Society of Jesus, the Oratory was entrusted with the direction of seminaries of Rachol and Chorão, though this direction was initially limited only to academic direction, while the Rectors and Vice-Rectors were still white ecclesiastics. This area of the Oratorian activity is awaiting further research.

The extinction of the Oratory took place when King Pedro of Portugal suppressed all religious Orders in Portugal and its overseas territories in retaliation for the ecclesiastical support given to his rival claimant Dom Miguel, in the civil war. The decree was issued in 1833, extended to the colonies in May 1834, and was carried out in Goa in 1835. Though the suppression was a pure act of reprisal, charges of degeneracy were brought as usual against all Orders.

Of the numbers that joined the Oratory, statistics are lacking. According to one source, there were about 66 Oratorians of Goa in the middle of the 18th century.[18] This number never seems to have exceeded 70s, and there were never more than 40 in Sri Lanka at any one time. At the time of the suppression, the total of the Oratorians was only 36.[19] On the extinction of the Oratory, its members in Sri Lanka placed themselves under the jurisdiction of *Propaganda Fide*. Rome soon detached Sri Lanka from the diocese of Cochin and constituted it into a Vicariate Apostolic, selecting one of the ex-Oratorians to be the first Bishop and Vicar Apostolic. However, Fr. Francis Xavier, who was nominated, died before the measure could be carried out. He was then replaced by another ex-Oratorian, Vincente do Rosario Dias. On his death in 1842, yet another ex-Oratorian, Cajetano Antonio was chosen by the Holy See. The last surviving Oratorian, Fr. Mathew Cajetano, was the Vicar General of two successive European Vicars Apostolic.

To conclude, let me quote the tribute paid by the great Sri Lankan historian of the Oratorians: "It (Cong. of Oratory) did for the Island what no other religious Order had done before or since".[20]

REFERENCES AND NOTES

1. Teotonio R. de Souza, "To the Nations and Nation", *Renovação* (Pastoral Bulletin of Goa Archdiocese), 15 February 1985, pp. 65-67.
2. C.R. Boxer, *Race Relations in the Portuguese Colonial Empire*, Oxford, 1963, p. 68.
3. In this present paper I have made extensive use of S.G. Perera, "The Congregation of the Oratory of Goa", *The New Review*, 1936, pp. 532-542.
4. V. Perniola, *The Catholic Church in Sri Lanka*, 7 vols. (1658-1795), Dehiwala, Tisara Prakashayo Ltd., 1983-91 (in progress).
5. Three editions of this are known. The first one of Lisbon (1745) is already too rare. The second edition by J.C. Barreto Miranda (Margão, 1867) is also hard to come by, and is valuable for its very useful annotations, as well as the additional "Sermon of the Holy Cross of Miracles" preached by Sebastião do Rego in 1745. A third edition was brought out by J.A. Ismael Gracias (1962) on the occasion of the 250th death anniversary of Fr. Joseph Vaz.
6. M. da Costa Nunes, *Documentação para a Historia da Congregação do Oratório de Santa Cruz dos Milagres do Clero Natural de Goa*, Lisbon, 1966, pp. ix-xiii.
7. J.M. do Carmo Nazareth, "Os religiosos da India e as bexigas", *O Oriente Portugues*, V, 1908, pp. 355-363.
8. J.B. Amancio Gracias. "Bens Pensionados de Goa", *O Oriente Portugues*, nos. 15-17 (New Series), 1937, pp. 193-238.
9. V. Perniola, *op. cit.*, III, p. xiv.
10. Carlos Merces de Melo, *The Recruitment and Formation of the Native Clergy in India, Lisbon*, 1955, pp. 129-177.
11. M. J. Gabriel de Saldanha, *Historia de Goa*, II, Panjim, 1926, p. 123, no. 1.
12. Perera, *Life of the Venerable Father Joseph Vaz*, Galle, 1953, pp. 17-28.
13. *Ibid.*, pp. 31-32.
14. *Ibid.*, pp. 37-38.
15. *Biblioteca Nacional* (Lisbon), Fundo General 176, fls. 149-153.
16. Saldanha, *op. cit.*, p. 110.
17. Perera, "The Congregation of the Oratorians of Goa", p. 538.
18. *Ibid.*, p. 539: Quotes from *Torre do Tombo* (Lisbon), Ms. Liv. 636.
19. Viriato A.C.B. de Albuquerque, "Congregaçäo do Oratorio de S. Filipe Nery em Goa", *O Oriente Portugues*, II, 1905, pp. 310-326.
20. Perera, *op. cit.*, p. 541.

[Published originally as "Oratorians of Goa, 1682-1835", *Goa: Cultural Trends*, ed. P.P. Shirodkar, Panjim, Goa, 1988, pp. 141-150].

5

XENDDI TAX:
A Portuguese Version of Jizya in Goa (1704-1841 A.D.)

The Portuguese empire overseas has been described as "a military and maritime enterprise cast in an ecclesiastical mould".[1] That it was military and maritime no one has ever questioned, but there have been conflicting opinions regarding the third qualification, i.e. ecclesiastical.[2]

It will not seem amiss to stress that the majestic dreams of the Portuguese monarchs received, at their request, Papal blessing and authorization to the effect that they might conquer and subdue Saracens, pagans, and all other unbelievers who were inimical to Christ and to Portuguese trade prospects.[3] The vast mass of contemporary State and ecclesiastical documents [4] entitle us to assert that "missionary harassment" was the hallmark of the Luso-Hindu relations in Goa during the 16th and 17th centuries.

Time and again the Portuguese authorities reminded themselves of the *leitmotiv* of their maritime enterprise, and consciously or unconsciously they respected the hierarchy of goals assigned to them by the Roman Pontiffs. The free hand given to the missionaries served only to dislocate trade,[5] and the excessive expenditure of public funds on religion contributed to the weakening of the entire fabric of the Portuguese "shoe-string" empire.[6]

The Portuguese in Goa levied a capitation-tax upon the Hindu as late as the 18th and 19th centuries. *It was called Pensão do Shendy.*[7] It was the last flicker of the flame of proselytism which burnt high in the previous centuries, and a symptom of the rapid decay of the Portuguese power.[8]

Missionaries against the Hindu 'Xenddi'

It was a strictly observed custom among the Hindus of Goa that every male child should undergo the ceremony of *zaival*[9] before he attained the age of five. A long braid of hair on the crown of their heads was a distinctive mark of the Hindus (of all castes), chiefly after the Christian missionary activity had begun to bear abundant fruit in Goa.

The first Ecclesiastical Council, which took place in Goa in 1567, marked the beginning of a systematic and relentless war against Hindu religious and social practices which were deemed harmful to the spiritual health of the new converts as occasions for relapse. The decrees of this and other subsequent Councils,[10] which received official State sanction, contained fulminations against such Hindu practices as, the worship of idols, the bearing of sandal marks on the body, the wearing of the sacred thread by the high-caste Hindus, and so on. It is surprising, however, that nowhere in these decrees do we find a single explicit reference banning the practice of growing *xenddi*. Nonetheless, much can be read between the lines.

The first Provincial Council decreed that no Christian should let himself be shaved by a non-Christian barber.[11] This prohibition cannot be explained merely by reference to the fact that barbers were the only surgeons of those days, and that their superstitious practices connected with that profession could harm the faith of their Christian patients. By way of justifying the prohibition, the same decree says: "on account of several inconveniences which follow" (*pelos incovenientes que disso se seguem*). What inconveniences could these be? It is very likely that the decree sought to prevent the new converts from looking at the barber working out the traditional *xenddi* pattern on the heads of their former brethern in faith. If the wearing of the sacred thread by Brahmins could scandalize the new converts and the Brahmins had to be told to hide the thread, [12] it is not improbable that the Hindus bearing *xenddi* and parading it all over could do great harm also.

The fifth and the last Provincial Council (1606) repeated the prohibitory order,[13] but this time it was extended to all persons, of whatever kind and condition they be. A fine of 50 *pardaus*[14] (about Rs. 25 in those days) was laid down against the defaulters. Like most of the other conciliar orders, this too appears to have failed in practice. The mere fact that the *xenddi* tax was levied about one century after the last Ecclesiastical Council forbade the practice, proves our point.

If in the case of the Council decrees we had to read between the lines, the contemporary Jesuit and private letters contain explicit and quite revealing information on the subject. The Jesuits were writing about their first-hand experience in dealing with Hindus whom they sought to convert to their Christian faith. Gaspar Dias, S.J. wrote to Portugal: "We gathered them all in one place after they had finished their meal. They wore braids of hair on their heads in keeping with their pagan custom. However, they are now ready to be reborn through water and through the Holy Spirit. Believe me. my brethern, my fingers and arms were paining after all the shaving I did".[15]

The following excerpt from a letter written by Sebastião Fernandes, S.J. depicts the intensity of the missionary hatred against the *xenddi* of the Hindus: "After a Hindu gentleman had consented to be baptized, a Jesuit Brother cut off his *xenddi*,which the boys there present hung on a tree and with much excitement and joy they stoned it and spat on it to the accompaniment of curses against pagan temples and idols".[16]

The truthfulness of the above reports is confirmed by a letter which Simão Botelho, the chief Revenue Comptroller of the *Estado da India*, sent to the King of Portugal. Denouncing the violent conversion methods employed by the Jesuits, he writes: "Besides other vexations and annoyances which they inflict upon the Hindus in order to constrain them to submit to being baptized, *forcibly shaved many of them,* and compelled them to eat flesh of cows and to sin against other of their superstitions and idolatrous rites".[17]

Introducing Xenddi Tax

It should be clear that this tax was imposed primarily as a fiscal measure, and only secondarily as a religious cess. At the close of the 17th century the plight of the Portuguese in India was not a happy one. Almost all their most valued possessions in the East had been wrested by the Dutch; the trade of the Portuguese had been by then almost entirely taken away from them by their more enterprising European rivals; the little maritime commerce which the Portuguese still maintained was being seriously disrupted by the Arab and other pirates that infested the Eastern seas; the Marathas had come to the fore as a fresh threat close at home; internally, the *Estado da India* was reduced to a condition of great depression and poverty, and it was torn asunder by the mean ambitions of the fidalgos and the intrigues of the friars; corruption was rampant at all levels of administration.[18] Added to these was the growing intolerance, as well as a bitter fanaticism of the Inquisition which kept up the sense of insecurity among the Hindus in Goa. The extent of harm it caused can only be guessed from the fact that Hindus had in their hands most of the local trade, and the local administration relied almost entirely on them for the collection of State revenues.[19]

Even though an empty treasury had become a chronic disease of the Portuguese administration all throughout the 17th century, the situation described above hastened the process and the State treasury hit rock-bottom at the close of that century. The authorities were hard at search for all possible sources of income to meet the ordinary expenses, and if possible to finance a campaign to reconquer Mombaça which had been lost to the Arabs in 1699.[20]

The Council of Public Revenue resolved at its meeting of September 26, 1701 to levy a land tax of 10% on the Portuguese, 5% on the natives, and 3% on the Province of the North, [21] for a period of three years. [22] However, the protests of the general village councils (*Camaras*) did not allow this levy to be put into execution. [23]

D. Caetano de Mello e Castro took over the administration of the *Estado da India* on October 5, 1702. He found that the administration was running at a deficit of 5,75,914 *xerafins*. [24] In order to remedy this situation, he summoned a meeting of the State Council, and despite a stiff opposition of the ecclesiastics, chiefly the Jesuits, he got a resolution passed which secured a land tax (*dizimos prediaes*) of 5% in Goa, Bardez and Salcete, [25] and of 3% in the Province of the North.[26] The victory of the Viceroy over the ecclesiastics proved to be of short duration. Their representations to the King brought out a Royal Decree (27 March, 1704) abolishing the new tax and asking the local authorities to find better substitutes, which ought to be "possible, proper, and proportionate to the capacity of the people, who should suffer neither oppression nor harm".[27]

On October 12, 1704 the Viceroy, D. Caetano de Mello de Castro assembled the State Council in order to find "mild" substitutes for the abolished tax, as required by the Royal Decree of March 27, 1704. At this meeting, the ecclesiastics were conspicious by their large number. There were more than a dozen of them: the Archbishop, who was a permanent member of the State Council; the Vicar General of the Dominican friars, [28] Antonio da Trindade; the Abbot of the Augustinian Convent, [29] Luis de Piedade; the Chief Commissioner of the Franciscans,[30] Lucas dos Remedios; the Provincial Superior of the Capuchins,[31] Joseph de Santa Maria; the official Visitor of the Jesuits to Goan Province,[32] Miguel de Amaral; the Provincial Superior of the Goan Jesuits, Andre Gomes; the delegate of the Rector of the Professed House of Bom Jesus[33]

Ignacio d'Andrade; the Prior of the Carmelites,[34] Leandro de S. Francisco Xavier; the Chief Commissioner of the Order of St. John of God[35] Antonio da Encarnação; the Treasurer of the Chapter of the Cathedral,[36] Canon Henrique Bravo de Moraes; and, a delegate to the same Chapter, Canon Luis Matozo da Cunha. They all formed a strong lobby whose view was bound to carry weight. As a rule, the ecclesiastics always joined hands to resist any move of the Government to tax their vast and ever increasing wealth. In this Council meeting (Oct. 12, 1704) the ecclesiastics were the first speakers. They were all unanimous in suggesting that the Hindus in Goa could be made to pay a certain annual contribution. They adduced the parallel of the Hindus who were subject to a heavy capitation tax in the neighbouring territory of the Mughuls.[37] Most of the other State authorities endorsed this proposal along with some other proposals. The Viceroy concluded the meeting by summing up the view of the majority which stood for four new levies: half quit-rents (*meyos foros*), a duty of one *xerafim*[38] on every *khandi*[39] of copra that might be exported, a duty of 5% on the sale of property (*meya ciza*), and a capitation tax upon the Hindus of Goa, Salcete and Bardez.[40]

Payment of Xenddi Tax

According to the Proceedings of the State Council, [41] the tax on *xenddi* was to be levied only on the Hindus whose distinctive trait it was, but Muslims were also subjected to its payment.[42]

The same resolution of the State Council which established the new tax, also fixed the amount that was to be paid by the individual non-Christians: The goldsmiths were to pay three *xerafins* per annum, the small shop-keepers (*botiqueiros*) three *xerafins* each, the brokers (*corretores*) also three *xerafins* each, the whole-sale traders (*mercadores*) five *xerafins* each, and all others working in any other profession would pay two *xerafins* each. [43]

The collection of this tax was left to the *mahajans*, [44] who took upon themselves the responsibility of drawing up the lists of the payers and of determining the quantum to be paid by each one. This method of collection seems to have given rise to severe extortions and abuses. The maximum payable had reached in some instances to fifty or even to hundred *xerafins*. These vexations led many to seek ways of evading the payment.[45]

In a letter[46] of 1718 the King informed the Viceroy Count of Ericeira that complaints had reached him from the Hindu inhabitants of two villages in the islands of Goa, namely Curca and Siridão, whereby they explained that they were required to pay twice the sum they paid earlier as *xenddi* tax.[47] The Viceroy wrote in reply: "The vexation about which the Hindus have complained to Your Majesty is common to all of them. The Hindu inhabitants of Curca and Siridão do not pay anything more than other Hindus, and if they be granted exemption, all others will have just reason to demand such favour.[48]

On October 26, 1731, the Hindus secured a provision from the Viceroy D. João de Saldanha da Gama granting them commutation of the *xenddi* tax. In future they would pay certain duties on the export of some commodities, such as one *tanga*[49] on one thousand coconuts, one *xerafim* on every *cumbo* [50] of salt, and half a *xerafim* on every *khandi*[51] of areca and copra. There was also a provision obliging the Hindus to pay an extra half *xerafim* on all the above commodities if the total collection did not make up the expected sum of 7,000 *xerafins* per year.[52] This concession was disapproved by the Council of Public Revenue on August 14, 1732.[53] It ordered that the *xenddi* tax should be paid by all Hindus and Muslims *(todo o gentio e mouro)* with the exception of those below the age of 15, the State interpreter (*o Lingoa do Estado*)[54] with his family and servants, and the umbrella-bearers (*porta-sombreiros*) [55] whose profession was regarded as lowly.

The Hindus never stopped devising ways and means of evading the payment of this tax. Some of them tried to interpret this tribute as due to the fact that Hindus had no immovable property (*bens de raiz*) and were thus free from many taxes which fell upon the property owners. Such were the quit-rents (*foros*), the tithes (*dizimos*) and the tax payable for the sale of property (*sizas*), none of which the Hindus paid. Even though the Hindus had made occasional substantial contributions to the State, their only regular and official contribution was this *xenddi* tax. Basing their action on this new interpretation, several Hindus made attempts to secure land and to win the privileges of *ganvkars*.[56] We have found a record of one such case in the Historical Archives of Goa. A certain Morguea Hegaddo and his son Azu Hegaddo claimed to be *ganvkars* of Margão[57] and, thus, exempt from the payment of *xenddi* tax.

In a letter to the King, dated January 9, 1734, the Viceroy Count of Sandomil wrote that there was a false understanding among the Hindus as regards the real motive which led to the imposition of the *xenddi* tax. Although erroneously, the Viceroy informed the King that the principal reason which led to the imposition of this tax was because of their religion, and the tax was named *xenddi* because that was the characteristic trait of their profession. It was not imposed because they possessed no immovable property. "If this argument is valid, we cannot explain why the Christians who do not have immovable property (and there are many such Christians) do not pay this tax. They should not be relieved of this payment unless they show willingness to accept our faith or decide to leave our territory, which they will not easily do, because they would be subject to greater extortions in the neighbouring territory".[58] We would regard the "principal reason" given by the Viceroy as an important one, but secondary. Just as some of the modern interpreters of Aurangzeb's administration tended to interpret his revival of jizya in 1679 as essentially a fiscal measure, which received an enthusiastic support of the theologians who infested his Court,[59] so also the xenddi tax was primarily a fiscal measure, but a measure suggested by the Religious bigots who infested the State Council.

From 1734 onwards, the Government dispensed with the services of the *mahajans* and decreed that the individuals concerned should make their payment directly to the Collector of the respective district. A time-limit was fixed to effect the payment and fines were laid down against those who failed to respect this time-limit.[60] The collection thereafter was done very smoothly, and the amount collected by way of *xenddi* tax had risen to c. 10,700 *xerafins* in 1734.

Extinction of Xenddi Tax

Tremendous changes had taken place in the political life of Portugal in the late 18th and early 19th centuries. Between 1750 and 1777, the enlightened rule of Marquis of Pombal brought about total overhauling of the administrative machinery and several other desirable changes.[61] He did away with the omnipotent influence of the Jesuits, secularized education and took pains to put an end to the social distinctions based on caste and class. Even though he did not abolish the hated Inquisition, which he used as a weapon to enforce his own plans and to fight his enemies, the changed situation had removed much of the wind from the inflated sails of Church influence in Goa. The repeated threats of the Marathas also served to reduce the heat of provocative measures against the Hindus.

The *xenddi* tax remained in force throughout the 18th century, and it was even extended to the New Conquests[62] after 1763.[63] Its final extinction had to wait for more changes to occur in the political scenario of Portugal. The ideas of the French Revolution and its spread by the

Napoleonic wars had the desired unsettling effect in Portugal. The forces of liberalism won their first victory in Portugal in 1822. Constitutionalism was firmly established. The Church was brought under State control and the Freemansons spread the new ideas of the freedom of belief.[64]

On December 12, 1840, the Governor General of the *Estado da India* issued an order abolishing the *xenddi* tax. The text of this order ran as follows: [65] "The hateful tribute, known as *xenddi* tax, which was imposed in 1705, is a cruel and ridiculous capitation tax befitting the times when it was established, but unbecoming of the ideas of the present century and of the spirit that guides the maternal government of Her Majesty, D. Maria, our Queen. This tribute brought in very little money, but was a source of many vexations to people. After hearing the views of the Council of Public Revenue, I thought it convenient to abolish this *xenddi* tax from the first day of the coming new year of 1841. This decree should be entered in the proper register and made known to all the authorities concerned and to people. Given at the Governor's Palace, Panjim, on the 22nd day of December, 1840". Signed J. J. Lopes de Lima.

Concluding Remarks

What follows is no final judgment, but just a few personal reflections provoked by the *xenddi* affair. We would describe it as a pathetic finale of a long-drawn drama which had begun with the arrival in Goa of the youthful and militant members of the Society of Jesus. They controlled the Royal Court in Portugal and threatened the Viceroys in India whenever the latter failed to be blind to the reality of the situation. By their financial acumen and abilities, the Hindus in Goa played the role of the Jews in Portugal. Almost all the tax-farmers (*rendeiros*) and the food-stuff suppliers to Goa were Hindus. The fanaticism of the religious must have too many times placed the Viceroys in embarassing situations. They dared not provoke the wrath of the Jesuits, but they just could not ignore the vital interests of the administration. Not rarely the Viceroys found a compromise solution by making exceptions in the anti-Hindu legislation they enforced. But if Portugal paid its debts to the Roman Pontiffs and did justice to its mission of Christianizing its overseas empire, it was not due to the persuasive methods favoured by its Indian administration, but due to the coercive policy championed by the Jesuits. But for the suppression of the Society of Jesus, the story of the *Xenddi* affair might have had some additional chapters.

REFERENCES AND NOTES

1. C.R. Boxer, *The Portuguese Seaborne Empire, p. 74; and Four Centuries of Portuguese Expansion*, pp. 18, 63.
2. A. D'Costa, *The Christianisation of the Islands of Goa; A. da Silva Rego, História das Missões do Padroado Português do Oriente — India*, I; C.R. Boxer, *A Note on Portuguese Missionary Methods in the East*; A.K. Priolkar, *The Goa Inquisition*. These and other works present different views on the Portuguese conquests by sword and cross.
3. F.M. da Costa Lobo, *A Acção Diplomática dos Portugueses nos séculos XV e XVI, destinada a realização de descobertas e conquistas*, Lisbon, 1937, pp. 106-7, 113, contian the texts of papal Bulls. Cf. Boxer, op. cit., pp. 20-23.
4. A. da Silva Rego, *Documentação para a história das Missões do Padroado Portugues do Oriente-India*, (12 vols.), Lisbon, 1947-55 ; J.H. da Cunha Rivara, *Archivo Portuguez-Oriental*, 6 fasc. in 10 vols., Panjim, 1857-76. New ed. of the Fasc.1 in 1877; Josef Wicki, *Documenta Indica* (18 vols.). Rome, *apud* "Monumenta Historica Soc. Jesu", 1948-1991.
5. A. Baião, *A Inquisição de Goa*, I, pp. 402-8; also Boxer, *op. cit.*, p. 270.
6. C.R. Boxer, *op. cit.*, p. xi.
7. Historical Archives of Goa (HAG): *Monções*, 102A, fl. 293v; *Documenta Indica*, VII, 301, no. 93; Dalgado, *Glossário Luso-Asiático*, 302, s.v. *Sendi. Xenddi* or *Xendim.*
8. We may also find a parallel to *xenddi* tax in the jizya of Aurangzeb's time.
9. A.B. de Brangança Pereira, *Etnografia da India Portuguesa*, pp. 274-275; Luis da Cunha Gonçalves, "Usos e Costumes dos habitantes não-cristãos da India Portuguesa", in *Estudos Coloniais*, Lisbon, 1948-49, I, Fasc. 2-3, 63.
10. Five ecclesiastical councils were celebrated in Goa (1567, 1575, 1585, 1592, 1606). The decrees of all these councils have been published by J.H. da Cunha Rivara in the Fasc. 4 of his *Archivo Portuguez* Oriental.
11. *Archivo Portuguez-Oriental*, IV, Panjim, 1862, p. 25: "...nenhum Christão se barbee com barbeiro infiel pelos inconvenientes que disso se seguem" (decree no. 29)
12. *Ibid.*, 124: See also p. 210 which in translation reads: "The past Councils had requested Your Majesty to ban among Your Hindu vassals the practice of wearing threads, because they do it after going through idolatrous rites. The way they wear these threads is scandalous to the new converts".
13. *Ibdi.*, p. 265.
14. R.J. de Lima Felner in *Subsídios para a História da India Portuguesa*, Lisbon, 1868, p. 62.
15. *Documenta Indica*, VII, doc. 63; pp. 272-303. Our excerpt occurs on pp. 301-302.
16. *Ibid.*, VIII, doc. 12, pp. 35-93. The excerpt is on p. 58.
17. Silva Rego, *Documentação*, V, p. 108.
18. F. C. Danvers, *The Portuguese in India*, II, 374-5; Meilink-Roelofsz, *Asia Trade and European Influence in the Indonesian Archipelago*. Ch. VI contains an interesting study of the Portuguese administrative vices in India.
19. *Archivo Portuguez-Orientiał* I, Part 2, 1876, pp. 57-58, 76-78, 93, 97-98, 104-106, 118-119, 191-192, 204; IV, 1862, pp. 24, 69, 73, 193; V, Part 2, 1865, pp. 748-749, 901-902; VI, Suppl. I: pp. 88-95, passim.
20. Boxer, *Four Centuries of Portugues Expansion*, p. 69.

21. Boxer, *The Portuguese Seaborne Empire*, p. 136: "The Province of the North comprised the Portuguese settlements along the sixty-mile stretch of the coast between Bombay and Daman. It extended for some twenty or thirty miles inland in some districts and it was the most productive part of what Indian territory was left to the Portuguese after their disastrous wars with the Dutch and the Omani". The headquarters for this province was Bassein -Ed.
22. HAG: *Assentos do Conselho do Estado*, vol. 7, fls. 27-2, 34-3.
23. J.B.A. Gracias, *Subsidios*, pp. 127-128.
24. *Xerafim or silver pardau* was equivalent to 5 *tangas or* 300 reis.
25. F.N. Xavier, *Bosquejo Historico das Communidades das Aldeas dos Concelhos das Ilhas, Salcete e Bardes* (4 parts), Panjim, 1852. Part II, pp. 1-4 contain historical notes relating to the conquest of Goa by Albuquerque in 1510, and the acquisition of Salcete and Bardez in 1543 by way of donation.
26. *Assentos do Conselho do Estado*, no. 7, fls. 49-57.
27. *Ibid.*, fls. 69-73.
28. Cottineau de Kloguen, *An Historical Sketch of Goa*. Reprinted by the Examiner Press, Bombay, 1910 as a Souvenir of the Exposition in Goa. *Vide*. pp. 77-80. The Order of Dominicans or Brother Preachers supplied six Archbishops to Goa. These religious preachers arrived in Goa soon after its conquest, but they did not have a convent until 1548.
29. *Ibid.*, pp. 80-3: The Augustinians were the fourth religious order established in Goa. They came to Goa in 1572. The half tower of their majestic Convent Church is still standing in Old Goa.
30. *Ibid.*,: It was the first order established in Goa, as its members were the chaplains of the first Portuguese vessels that came out to India. The Convent of St. Francis of Assisi which belonged to them today houses the Archaeological and Survey Department of the Government of Goa.
31. *Ibid.* The Capuchins or Friars Minor were a reformed branch of the Franciscans.
32. St. Francis Xavier, the founder-member of the Society of Jesus came down to Goa on May 6, 1542. He established the Society in Goa and gave a boost to the conversion movement. The Jesuits played an important role in the early history of Goa, and they were feared even by the Viceroys. The Society of Jesus was banned by Marquis of Pombal in 1759. The following year Jesuits of Goa were packed and sent to jails in Portugal.
33. It is a Minor Basilica which houses the Holy remains of St. Francis Xavier. The façade of this Church is a fine specimen of the Portuguese Baroque-Manueline architecture.
34. Cottineau, *op.cit.* It was a reformed branch of the Carmelites, known as bare-footed Carmelites (*descalços*) that established a Convent in Goa in 1607.
35. *Ibid.*, 87: This order of Religious Brothers came to Goa about the 17th century. They looked after the sick in the hospitals, and even today their Convent and Church are used to house the aged.
36. *Ibid.* The Cathedral or the Metropolitan Church in Goa was a small Chapel when Albuquerque first ordered its building. It was made a Cathedral in 1543. Today it stands as a majestic edifice with one tower only.
37. *Assentos do Conselho do Estado*, no. 7, fls. 69-73.
38. See n. 49 below.
39. A. Nunes, *Lyuro dos Pesos da Ymdia, in Subsidios*, p. 31. *Candis* 20 *maunds* = 480 pounds and = 3 quintals, 3 *arrobas*. 1 Arroba = 32 *arratels* or pounds avd.
40. *Assentos do Conselho do Estado, loc. cit.*

41. V. T. Gune, *Assentos do Conselho do Estado: A Detailed Subject-Index and a Table of Contents in Brief.* Panjim, 1972.
42. HAG: *Assentos do Conselho da Fazenda*, vol. 21, fls. 247-250; Monçöes, 102A, fls. 282-284v, 293v-294v.; *Assentos do Conselho do Estado*, no. 7, fls. 69-73.
43. *Assentos do Conselho do Estado, loc. cit.*
44. They were the founders of temples and upkeepers of religious cult. There were corporations of *mazanes*. *Cf.* C. A. B. de Brangança Pereira, "*Etnografia da India Portuguesa*". II, p. 227; Ponciano J.M. de Souza, *Indice Alphabetico. Chronologico e Remissivo*, p. 302 has coordinated government legislation on mazanias.
45. HAG: *Monções* 102A, fl. 294.
46. *Archivo Portuguez Oriental*, VI. Suppl. 2 (1876), doc. 22.
47. The collection from these villages in 1786 is recorded as 82 *xerafins*.
48. *Archivo Portugues Oriental*, VI, Suppl. 2, doc. 22.
49. *Tanga* was equivalent to 60 reis, and five *tangas* went into the making of *a xerafin*. A *tanga* was also equivalent to 4 *barganys*. *Cf. Hobson-Jobson* v.s. *Tanga* and *Bragany*.
50. A.B. de Bragança Pereira, "Etnografia da India Portuguesa", in *A India Portuguesa*, Panjim, 1923, pp. 253-523. *Cumbo* = 20 *candis* = 400 *curos* = 3194,4 *litres*.
51. *Supra*, n. 39.
52. HAG: *Monções* 102A, fl. 282.
53. HAG: *Assentos do Conselho da Fazenda*, no. 21, fls. 247-250.
54. Pissurlencar, *Agentes da Diplomacia Portuguesa na India*, Bastora, 1952, p. 80.
55. This was the class of Boias who also carried palanquins which was a favourite means of transport among the respectable citizens of Goa from the seventeen to the nineteenth centuries.
56. F.N. Xavier, *op. cit.*, II, 1-4, no. 3.
57. HAG: *Justificações*, Ms. 9528. fls. 106-11.
58. HAG: Monções 102A, loc.cit.
59. S.R. Sharma, The Religious Policy of the Moghul Emperors, Bombay, 1962, 153, 175.
60. HAG: Monço~es, loc.cit.
61. J. Ferreira, *Historia de Portugal*, pp. 567-622.
62. F.C. Danvers, *op. cit.* on p. 429; Pissurlencar, Roteiro, note on pp. 103-104. The Novas Conquistas were provinces occupied after 1763: Pernem, Bicholim, Satari, Ponda, Embarbacem, Astrgar, Bali, Chandravaddi, Cacora, Canacona, and Cabo da Rama.
63. Ponciano J.M. de Souza, *op. cit.*, p. 497, s.v. Xendim.
64. João Ameal, *Historia de Portugal*, Porto, 1958, 4th ed., pp. 617-47.
65. HAG: *Portarias do Governo*,, fl. 35.

[Was originally published as "*Xenddi* Tax: A Phase in the History of Luso-Hindu Relations in Goa, 1704-1841 A.D.", *Studies in the Foreign Relations of India: From the earliest times to 1947* (Prof. H.K. Sherwani Felicitation Volume), ed. P.M. Joshi and M.A. Nayeem, Hyderabad, 1975, pp. 463-471.]

6

A GOAN COUNTRY-TRADING AND AGENCY HOUSE : The Mhamay Sarkar

On the occasion of the first International Seminar of Indo-Portuguese History in 1978 I had made an appeal through my paper entitled "The Voiceless in Goan Historiography"[1] for a radical shift in the trend of Goan history writing from the past politically orchestrated or tourism-oriented presentation of "Golden Goa". My *Medieval Goa*[2] was published the next year (1979) as a token of personal contribution to the programme of re-writing the history of Goa by replacing the colonial history with a history of the common person, or by substituting the bourgeois interest in "Golden Goa" with a concentration on socio-economic pressures and opportunities to which the Goan population was awakened by the Portuguese rule. I repeat my tune at the second International Seminar of Indo-Portuguese History, not with any fanatic fervour of nationalism or anti colonialism, but only to press for a new and rectified historiography that will take care of past deficiencies of *approach and evidence.* History of the Portuguese *Goa-based* empire needs to be truly *Indo-Portuguese.* The new approach that I have been advocating will alone make such historiography relevant to the people of the areas concerned in the context of their new aspirations, new prospects, new challenges. Search for, and utilization of, indigenous *evidence* alone can help to reduce over-dependance on colonial European documentation and to write an Indo-Portuguese history from the inside.

Like all colonial powers, also the Goa-based Portuguese empire was established and maintained with significant assistance of the local population. If this assistance was not motivated by selfish interests of the native groups, it was forced out of them. The recent writings of M.N.

Pearson,[3] A.R. Disney,[4] G.V. Scammell,[5] as well as my own,[6] have laid sufficient stress on the important role played by the Saraswat Brahmins in the Portuguese Goa-based economy. This vital assistance in revenue administration and commercial life is awaiting a more detailed and satisfactory treatment with the help of documentation that needs to be procured beyond official archives. The revenue farmers kept their own registers of tax-payers and tax-payment, and the business houses definitely kept minute records of their activity. The late Prof. Pissurlencar, celebrated archivist-historian of Goa, brought to light private family papers of the non-Christian State interpreters in his *Agentes da Diplomacia Portuguesa na India*,[7] illustrating profusely the role played by the natives in Indo-Portuguese diplomacy. Similar effort is yet to be undertaken to illustrate native assistance or resistance to Indo-Portuguese economy.

The new approach and the new evidence may give an impression that I am consciously or unconsciously identifying Indo-Portuguese historiography with Goan historiography. This is not so, even if the history of a Goa-based empire needs to be Goan to some extent. The new-data cache made up of nearly 60,000 loose papers and 250 codices is replete with information on *carreira* and *cabotagem*[8] from the last quarter of 18th century to the end of the first quarter of 19th century, covering the trade network that extended from Lisbon and Brazil to Bengal and China. This information contains many details on the so-called "country trade" with the Asian and African ports west and east of Cape Comorin.[9] The involvement of the Mhamai family in slave and opium trade during the above-mentioned period is bound to arouse the interest of researchers whose interest in Goan history or Indo-Portuguese history is only marginal. Hence, our new approach and evidence seeks to make Indo-Portuguese historiography more relevant and attractive to Indians without making it less attractive and relevant to those outside India.

Camotim Mamay Family: Background History and Legends

Camotim is the Portuguese version of the native *Kamat*, a family name that designated a particular hereditary function exercised in the village-community set-up. Kamat headed a traditional association (*bhaus*) of peasants who cultivated the reclaimed lands (*khazans*) which needed cooperative labour to protect them against inundations by taking regular care of the protective clay-levees and sluice-gates.[10] Hence, one could find Kamat families wherever there were large areas reclaimed for paddy cultivation. Caste-wise they happen to be always Brahmins, which goes to suggest the important role played by this caste not only in the socio-political organization of the country but even in agricultural development in the difficult times of initial settlement.

In the wake of the conversion drive in Goa in mid-16th century several Brahmin families opted for loss of their landed rights and privileges instead of betraying their ancestral faith.[11] However, they proved their ability to exploit the new situation to their best advantage. The development of Goa as an important trading and commercial centre, as well as the needs of the colonial administration provided them with ample opportunities to make good their economic losses in spite of the discriminating legislation on religious grounds. [12] One such piece of legislation which denied to non-Christians the right to own land-property in Goa may have been provided the strongest incentive to keep re-investing their growing capital in business. [13] Among the Saraswat Brahmin families which thus prospered amidst adversity there were many *Camotins.*

Farming of revenue-collection rights in the Portuguese jurisdiction of Goa had become almost an exclusive business of Saraswat Brahmins, predominantly Sinays. The Portuguese administration could not help depending on their knowledge of local usages, and these natives exploited to the utmost this profit-making profitably in trade and commerce. We do not come across *Camotins in* the books of revenue administration until the mid-17th century,[14] but before mid-18th century some Camotins had already risen to remarkable financial power. In the wake of anti-Hindu feelings whipped up in Goa during the Maratha invasion of the territory in 1739 the city rabble was provoked by some clerical leaders to mob the house of Phondu Kamat, the wealthiest merchant of Goa under the pretext of having sheltered some enemies. In addition to much that he lost in this mob-attack, the State demanded from him alone 1,30,000 *xerafins* to pay for the retreat of the invading Maratha forces.[15] Most probably it is the same house being administered in 1770 by Bhagvatiny Camotiny, widow of Raulu Camotim, addressing a representation to the Crown on behalf of her house which she describes as "the most important business house of the city of Goa and greatly involved in the seaborne trade of the empire". In the said representation we read that during the earthquake of Lisbon the family lost a consignment of goods worth 96,000 *xerafins*, and that with the suppression of the Society of Jesus the family was left unpaid a debt of 2,03,370 *xerafins* which the Jesuits of China owed it.[16] The Goan administrator-historian Felipe Nery Xavier has also recorded curious details of the grandeur of the house of Rucuminim Camotinim, which he classifies as the first of the three most important business houses of Goa in the last quarter of the 18th century.[17]

It is not possible to identify the various Kamat families merely on the basis of the documentary references available. Hence, it is not possible to identify the ancestry of the Camotim family to whom the present "Mhamai Family Records" belong, unless they use their additional distinguishing - *Mhamay*. One would need to check extensively on oral tradition to reconstruct the links otherwise. The earliest reference to the distinguishing surname "Mamay" that I could find was in a loose document of the Historical Archives of Goa dating back to 1781. It is a petition of the Hindu businessmen of Goa requesting the Crown to lift the ban on the public celebration of their weddings with their customary ceremonies. They quote the precedent of some prominent businessmen, such as Suba Camotim Mamay, who were granted such permission during the viceroyalty of Ega (1756-65).[18]

The additional surname assumed by this Camotim family derived from the family deity *Mahamaya* which was an important deity of Guirdolim village in Salcete taluka of Goa according to the recorded traditions of Saraswat Brahmins in *Konkanakyana*. [19] According to the oral traditions maintained in the family the Camotins of Guirdolim left the village to escape the conversion-drive in mid-16th century and sought shelter in the neighbouring Sunda territory. The family deity was established for a long time at a place called Shiroti at Cabo da Rama, from where they wanted to bring it to Kundaim in the Phonda taluka in mid-18th century, but the bearers of the deity's statue were unable to proceed beyond Fatorpa. The deity was then established there itself under a banyan tree and for that reason came to be known as *Vadd-devata*.[20] The decision to shift may have been motivated by the fact that other big temples were being erected in the Phonda taluka, which was just across the Portuguese jurisdiction of Goa and not too far for the devotees engaged in the business of Goa to frequent.[21] Suba Camotim already mentioned earlier was probably established in Goa before he shifted his residence to Panjim around the time when the Count of Ega shifted the viceregal palace to this suburban village (1759). He was appointed one of the four official brokers of the Goa Customs in 1757,[22] and he died before November 1765. His widow, Subadry Comotiny, brother Custam, and sons, Vencatesha, Naraena and Yeshwant, were still repaying in 1778 the debt of 32,000 *xerafins* contracted by Suba in 1760 from the Royal Hospital.[23]

The three sons of Suba had established themselves as a joint family trust (*sarkar*) which was administered in the name of Vencatesha and Naraena. Their brother Yeshwant or Exa took care of the business in Bombay till his death in 1815. [24] The business or other activities of Vencatesha find references in the records of the Goa Historical Archives, but one can get only a limited idea of the full involvement of these Mhamais because of the sporadic occurrence of such references as well as due to incompleteness of the information they offer. The same could be said of every other Hindu family of Goa whose private records alone could help to reconstruct satisfactorily a detailed story of the role they played in the destiny of the colonial rulers and subjects. We are fortunate to have the family records of the Mhamais (donated to the Xavier Centre of Historical Research by the historian-son of the family and my good friend Dr. S. K. Mhamai) that can enable us to get an insight into the extent and intensity of the economic control exercised by the natives in the Portuguese eastern empire. Historians of the empire have long smelt this silent and ellusive control suggested by the recorded comments of some observant comtemporaries. Thus, for instance, we know of Dom Manuel Lobo de Silveira, who was in close touch with the Goa administration for over half a century in the latter part of the 17th century, having told his fellow councillors of State that the Hindu businessmen took away all the butter and fat from the Portuguese and the Canarins as they monopolized Goa's entire export trade and also acted as monopolists and engrossers in the retail trade of Goa, charging what prices they liked, and hoarding what they could not sell. [25] Beyond such observations the observant contemporaries themselves must have been at a loss at piercing deeper the shrewd workings of the financial underworld. It is my hope that with the help of the Mhamai Papers historians of the Portuguese colonial empire will be able to go beyond sniffing, and lift to some extent the prevailing veil of secrecy.

Mhamai House Papers

Back in 1977 I wrote a brief study on "Marine Insurance and Indo-Portuguese Trade History", [26] and there I mentioned passingly that any surviving papers of the Mhamai family could be of help for a better understanding of the subject. A year later, Dr. Mhamai, archivist at the Goa Historical Archives gave a brief description of the nature of their family papers in a paper that he contributed to *Sources of the History of India.*[27] This confirmed my hopes, but neither I nor the man of the family himself had any clear idea of the bulk of the surviving records. This may surprise the reader who has no idea of the functioning of the historic Mhamai mansion in the vicinity of the Government Secretariat in Panjim (Goa). It is an old sprawling, two-floored, structure with long corridors and halls and over thirty-five living rooms set around two internal courtyards and occupied by over sixty old and young people, belonging to different families of the Mhamai clan. Few in the family have any clear idea about the vast and scattered common belongings. The records were lying in loose bundles, boxes, trunks, in most unexpected nooks and corners of the residence. And these were only the papers that stayed behind after a family friend and antiquarian, Mr. Angle, had taken away nearly a cart-load of them to study the history of the Mhamai family. The man died before he could proceed far with his hobby and no one could trace the records he had taken.

The papers that have been salvaged and are now at the XCHR are being classified and made available to scholars. In addition to financial and technical problems of preservation, the language of the documents is a major hurdle. Three-fourths of the papers are written in old Kannada script (*Kandevi* script), and rare are the scholars who can tackle it. [28] A sizable number of the papers are in Modi, and many others are in Gujarati and Sanskrit. There are just two papers in Persian, which happen to be deeds of obligation to repay cash borrowed by Sayed Zainul Abedin Khan from the Mhamais in 1781 during his visit to Goa on his way to Isle de France to secure French military assistance for the Marathas against the English.[29]

The papers in European languages form about a third of the total amount, and these have been classified into four categories, namely: 1. Incoming Correspondence (in Portuguese, French, and English); 2. *Borradores* or Draft-Books of Outgoing Correspondence (in Portuguese and French); 3. Books of Accounts of commercial transactions and farmed revenues (in Portuguese, French and English); and 4. Copies of Judicial Proceedings (in Portuguese).

The present report is based on my first reading of much of the incoming correspondence and drafts of the outgoing. Hence, this may be considered only as a trailor of a more elaborate study that we have hope for from someone qualified to unravel the mysterious contents of the numerous account books and ledgers written in *Kandevi* script. The following thematic arrangement of my report takes care only of the issues that my reading of the papers spotted out as salient or curious, but it need not be considered as adequate or even as fairly exhaustive. It is aimed only at arousing some interest in the researchers of Indo-Portuguese history to take advantage of every new bit of relevant evidence that surfaces, including these Mhamai Papers.

1. *State Revenue Farmers*

Even though Suba Camotim Mamay had got himself selected and appointed as an official broker at the Customs in 1757, he did not lay the foundations of the family business with the earnings of this job alone. He sought a loan form the Administration of the "*Confisco*" (confiscated property) of the suppressed Society of Jesus, and also sought to build his capital by joining the club of revenue-farmers. There is a complaint lodged against Suba Camotim by his two brothers, Upea and Pandu, in connection with a lease of three Crown lands that he held in Colvale (Bardez).[30] His son Vencatesha is known to have been a revenue farmer of Mahem (Bicholim taluka), Talavarda and county of Cuncolim-Veroda (in Salcete taluka) for many years after 1798. [31]

The Mhamai brothers had also taken up farming of tobacco revenue which had become an important source of State revenue at the time.[32] If the administration of revenue helped many to accumulate capital and rise further, it must have also caused the downfall of many who who were unfortunate to find some State officials unwilling to connive at their methods of accounting. The Mhamais met such a fate with the arrival of the Viceroy Count of Rio Pardo, whose earnestness in checking abuses in various branches of administration caught the Mhamai brothers on the wrong foot. They were declared debtors to the State to the tune of 180,000 and plus *xerafins* in 1818. With their properties confiscated, goods and credits mortgaged and frozen, the Mhamai family began experiencing symptoms of decline and never fully recovered its prosperity of the first decade of the 19th century. [33]

2. *Provision-Suppliers and Shipyard Contractors*

The earliest papers of the collection dating back to 1759 refer to Suba Camotim attending to the furnishing and provisioning of Viceroy's new palace at Panjim. There are codices with details of this function exercised by the Mhamai family till 1811. They also supplied the needs of the State shipyard by taking care of State and private vessels that came in for wintering or needed refitting and provisioning before sailing away. This job provided the Mhamais an excellent opportunity to further their interests in many ways: They became much wanted contact men and supply agents with investments in the *carreira* and *cabotagem*, and that is how we come across letters with constant requests seeking passports, gun-pieces from State shipyard, goods for export,[34] and such other forms of assistance which the Mhamais were in a good position to render with their close contacts with the administrative quarters. The Mhamais made good use of their position to function almost as a parallel government to promote their own interests and the interests of their partners and well-wishers.[35] It may be noted that the Mhamais extended their technical assistance to areas beyond Goa. Owners of vessels caught in storms or taken by coastal pirates sought their help. We know of a big salvage-operation undertaken by the Mhamais off the coast of Mangalore where the ship *Ceilão Novo* went down in 1807.

3. *Brokers and Insurers*

The Mhamai brothers continued their father's job of official broker at the Goa Customs. Many papers related to this function give us an idea of the nature of goods that entered Goa by different routes, as well as their prices and duties levied. This position made the Mhamais popular among the businessmen who depended on their good services, and in turn gave the Mhamais certain leverage in the trade network. In addition to broker's services which they extended to all and sundry, the Mhamais acted as official brokers of the French in Goa. In this capacity they attended to the needs of the visiting Frenchmen and French ships, and acted as money lenders and political informers. It is shocking to note that hardly a single researcher of the French colonial adventure in India has been able to identify this family in Goa. The family papers include extensive correspondence with inportant French officials and businessmen, like Saint-Lubin, Montigny, Warnet, Monneron, Picot, *et al.* The use of these records may shed more light on the political intrigues of the French to survive in India.[36]

As said earlier, it was in connection with a study on maritime insurance that my attention was first drawn to Mhamai records. They provide information of this nature. In 1790 they sought insurance for the ship *Sacramento* that left Goa for Timor and would return via Batavia. It was insured for Rs. 25,000 in Surat by a group of merchants for an interest of 5.25%.[37] There is reference to insurance done also in Surat for Rs. 40,000 when the ship *Marquez de Angeja* left for Lisbon in 1798.[38] In 1807 they had insured goods aboard *N. S. dos Milagres e Beleza do Mar* that was leaving Goa for Moçambique via Daman carrying forty casks and one box of beads valued at Rs. 20,000. The risk was underwritten by a group of merchants. They had been contacted by the Mhamais through their Bombay-based agents and on behalf of a Lisbon merchant, Francisco Xavier de Maia.[39] There are details that could lead to a better knowledge of the direction, quality and volume of trade, trade organization, and many curious incidents concerning natural hazards, political threats, piracy, smuggling, etc. Thus a Surat-based Portuguese businessman, Jacinto Domingues was writing to the Mhamais in 1793 that the news of the outbreak of the peninsular war had made it impossible for him to get anyone to accept insurance for goods valued over Rs. 4,00,000 which he and his friend had for dispatching to Timor and China.[40]

4. *Dealers in Slaves and Opium*

Trading in slaves and opium may look immoral and objectionable, but they had their peak days. Drug-peddling is not unknown today! The Mhamai records are quite informative about the movement of Negro slaves through Goa. Their clients were mostly Frenchmen of the Isle of France.[41] Many of the slaves reached other destinations, such as Macau and Ceylon. Sir Roger de Faria's correspondence with the Mhamais is interesting. [42] The Goan businessman in Bombay had made a fortune with opium trade and counselled the Mhamais not to soil their conscience by trading in rice and slaves (*cujo ganho e proveito sempre leva mau fim como tenho visto, e arruina muita gente*).[43]

To conclude it is our ardent hope that even this sketchy picture of the Mhamais will motivate greater use of indigenous sources for writing Indo-Portuguese history.

REFERENCES AND NOTES

1. T.R.de Souza, "The Voiceless in Goan Historiography", *Indo-Portuguese History: Sources and Problems*, Bombay, 1981, pp. 114-131.
2. De Souza, Teotonio, R., *Medieval Goa*, New Delhi, 1979.
3. M.N. Pearson, "Indigenous Dominance in a Colonial Economy: the Goa Rendas, 1600-70", *Mare Luso-Indicum*, II, Paris, 1973.
4. A.R. Disney, "The Portuguese Empire in India c. 1550-1650: Some Suggestions for a Less Seaborne, More Landbound Approach to Its Socio-Economic His-

tory", *Indo-Portuguese History: Sources and Problems*, Bombay, 1981, pp. 148-162.

5. G. V. Scammel, "Indigenous Assistance in the Establishment of Portuguese Power in Asia in the Sixteenth Century", *Modern Asian Studies*, XIV, 1980, pp. 1-11.
6. T. R. de Souza, "Glimpses of Hindu Dominance of Goan Economy in the Early Seventeenth Century", *Indica* XII, 1975, pp. 27-35; "Goa-based Portuguese Seaborne Trade in the Early Seventeenth Century", *The Indian Economic and Social History Review*, XII, 1975, pp. 433-442; "Marine Insurance and Indo-Portuguese Trade History: An Aid to Maritime Historiography", *The Indian Economic and Social History Review*, XIV, no. 3, 1977, pp. 377-384.
7. P.S.S. Pissurlencar, *Agentes da Diplomacia Portuguesa na India*, Bastora, 1952.
8. *Carreira da India* was the round trip between Lisbon and India; *Cabotagem* was the coastal trade.
9. "Country trade" was the expression in vogue from the end of the 17th century to the middle of the 19th century. Broadly speaking it included trade both by Indians and Europeans residing in India. Cf. N.H. Coates, *The Old Country Trade of the East Indies*. London, 1911; Pamela Nightingale, *Trade and Empire in Western India, 1784-1806*, Cambridge, 1970.
10. De Souza, T.R., *Medieval Goa*, p. 63.
11. A. D'Costa, *The Christianisation of the Goa Islands*, Bombay, 1965, pp. 111, 119; A.K. Priolkar, The Goa Inquisition. Bombay, 1961, pp. 61ff, 114ff.
12. De Souza, *op. cit.*, pp. 118-19.
13. HAG: *Monções* 58, fl. 365; *Monções* 59, fl. 27-28; T.R.de Souza, "Xenddi-Tax: A Phase in the History of Luso-Hindu Relations in Goa, 1704-1841", *Studies in the Foreign Relations of India*, Hyderabad, 1975, p. 467.
14. HAG: Ms. 1371, *Fianças*, no. 3, fls. 33v, 94, 99, 132, 190.
15. Pissurlencar, *The Portuguese and the Marathas*, ed. P.R. Kakodkar, Bombay, 1975, pp. 276-281, 302.
16. AHU: India, *Maço* 1, doc. 46.
17. F.N. Xavier, *Additamento ao Codigo dos Usos e Costumes*, Panjim, 1861, 21, no. 5.
18. HAG: Loose and unclassified doc. dated 24th March 1781. Cf. Priolkar, *op. cit.*, pp. 118-121.
19. V. Wagle, *Konkanakhyana*, Bombay, 1909, p. 13.
20. Loc. cit.
21. V.N. Dhume, *Shri Mangesha Devasthan*, Margão, 1971, p. 89; *Golden Goa*, Bombay, Marg Publication, 1980, p. 91.
22. HAG: Ms. 1578, *Portarias do Governo*, no. 3, fl. 105.
23. XCHR: Mhamai House Records.
24. *Ibid.*, Letter of Francisco Antonio de Carvalho, Bombay, 21.7.1815.
25. C.R. Boxer, *Portuguese India in the Mid-Seventeenth Century*, New Delhi, 1980, p. 43.
26. T.R. de Souza, "Marine Insurance in Indo-Portuguese Trade History", *The Indian Economic and Social History Review*, XIV, no. 3, 1977, pp. 377-384.
27. S.K. Mhamai, "Portuguese and the Mhamai Family of Goa", *Sources of the History of India*, I, ed. S.P. Sen., Calcutta, 1978, pp. 453-456.
28. G. Ghantkar, *An Introduction to Goan Marathi Records in Halakanada Script*. Margão, 1973. The book includes a specimen document from the Mhamai collection. [As this book goes into print Mr. Ghantkar has come out with his

enlarged version of research entitled *History of Goa through Gõykanadi Script* (Panjim, 1993) with a wider selection of old Goan records in Kannada script. This volume will be a boon for scholars and will certainly throw fresh light on the rural life. I wish to recall my personal gratitude to Mr. Ghantkar, whose help in using some such material enabled me to present a better picture of Goan rural life in my *Medieval* Goa, which was my doctoral work published in 1979.]

29. S.P. Sen, *The French in India*, New Delhi, 1971, p. 201. Zainul Abedin did not proceed further from Goa where he happened to meet the French envoy Montigny, Oct. 1781.
30. HAG: Ms. 1157, *Petições Despachadas do Conselho da Fazenda*, fl. 39.
31. HAG: Ms. 2281, *Registos Gerais da Fazenda*, fls. 292v, 302v-305; XCHR: Mahamai House Records, Account Books of the Administration of Cuncolim-Veroda County, 1810-1814.
32. Silva Rego, (ed.), *Documentação Ultramarina Portuguesa*, V, Lisbon, 1967. Contains much information on tobacco revenue in 1770s.
33. M.V. de Abreu, *O Governo do Vice-Rei Conde do Rio Padro*, Panjim, 1869, p. 120, doc. 46.
34. XCHR: Mhamai House Records.
35. M. Gadkari, "Indrache Tatt: Govyantil Don Sarkaren", *Gomantak*, Panjim, 5th Sept, 1971, p. 1.
36. S.P. Sen *op. cit.* Even this comparatively recent and one of the best studies of the French in India contains no mention of Mhamai family.
37. XCHR: Mhamai House Records — Letter from Surat, dated 7.4.1790.
38. XCHR: Mhamai House Records — Letter of Francisco Gomes Loureiro from Surat, dated 31.8.1798.
39. The following businessmen had accepted the insurance: Nasserwanjee Cowasjee, Lalubai Duarcadas, Rustamjee Beiramjee, Givajee Mervanjee, Narsindas Purxotamdas, G. D'Mello, Vishwanath Ramohandas Dalvi, Calian Tacarsy, Baidas Quessurdas, Lerachand Panechand, Tacarshy Vacatchand, Galatchand Nanabhoy, Tapidas Amratlal, Minguel de Lima e Souza, Nicolau de Lima e Souza, Rozario de Quadros, and J.F. Pereira and Ca.
40. XCHR: Mhamai House Records — Letter of Jacinto Rodrigues from Surat dated 4.7.1793.
41. *Cf.* docs. I & III in the Appendix.
42. XCHR· Mhamai House Records — Letters of Roger de Faria, Bombay, 2.5.1809, and 20.9.1812 referring to dispatch of slaves by the Mhamais to his friends in Macao and Ceylon.
43. A.M. da Cunha, *Sir Roger de Faria*, Panjim, 1928; R.F. Vachha, *Mumbai No Bahar*, I, Bombay, 1874, pp. 235-237; M. Greenberg, *British Trade and the Opening of China, 1800-42*, Cambridge, 1951, pp. 124-125, 134; XCHR: Mhamai House Records — Letter of Roger Faria dated 11.10.1812. The quoted Portuguese lines means: "The gain and profit from it always has a bad end and causes downfall of many".

APPENDIX-I

Letter from Couronat to Narayan [1] Camotim, Poona, 15.X.1777 (Summary in English)

Acknowledges receipt of a letter dated 26th August. Promises to send within four to five days a person of confidence with Rs. 20,000 for purchase of slaves and ivory.

Gives specifications of goods required: young and strong Negro-slaves; half of them adult males, one-fourth females, and the rest young males. All should be healthy and without defects. Whatever the cost, wants two male slaves who can sound horns, and two young and graceful females..

Wishes to visit Goa with a lakh and half to two within a month. Will bring along anchors, ropes, canons, and some guns, and expects help to dispose these goods quickly.

Wants that no news of these transactions should reach the ears of the ambassador. Complains that a Brahmin relation of the Camotins at the Poona court passes on information to the ambassador. Does not want this to continue happening with his affairs.

The ambassador, that is, the French envoy at Poona, owes him money and is in bad terms with him presently.

APPENDIX-II

Reply of Narayan Camotim to Mr. Couronat. Goa, 1.XI.1777 (Summary in English)

Acknowledges the letter of 15th Oct. 1777. Has begun looking for slaves and is awaiting the man with money. Promises to deal with the matter as a personal interest.

Informs that a month back Mr. Galinem had come from Mauritius[2] and took 160 slaves. Presently Mr. Larochet was in Goa with his ship for taking 140 slaves. The ship from Mozambique had arrived on 28th September with about 700 slaves.

Informs that less ivory had come than in previous years. However he had instructed his agents in Daman to look for a better deal in ivory there. Is awaiting his arrival and has rented storage place and is looking out for prospective buyers.

Disclaims any family relationship with the Brahmin at the Poona court and says that he was only an accquaintance from Bombay whom he had instructed to assist Couronat.

Advises not to bring guns to Goa if they can be disposed more profitably elsewhere. Informs that ships from Portugal have not yet arrived.

APPENDIX-III

Letter of João da Silva Guedes to Vencatesha and Narayana Camotim.Mozambique, 22nd August, 1800 (Summary in English)

Has sent a letter by the Daman ship in April informing that goods consigned to Justice Manoel Jose Gomes Loureiro have been accepted.

Has sold some piece-goods and wheat and invested the income in gold remitted by the vessel *Veiga Cabral* as indicated in the receipts and accounts that are going along.

Pitch and sugar-candy can be sold, but tea is definitely unwanted due to its inferior quality, and also due to the glut caused by large supplies that have come from different places. Will try to dispose of it after the monsoon.

The ship *Balsemão* arrived on 16th June and had orders from Messers. Francos of Lisbon to hand over guns to the supercargo of the same ship. The man has refused to take them, because they were 20 boxes or so, and he feels that they may not find a good market on the Indian coast. He prefers to leave them behind and save the owners the freight expenses. They will be kept in the godowns of the Customs House. There was another consignment of guns belonging to another businessman of Lisbon, which he gave on the order of the owner to the super cargo the previous year, and he had returned them after having been loaded, advising him to sell them for a *pataca* and half each, if he could. He had to allow the buyers to bargain even further.

This happens because of the slump in the slave-trade, and there is no demand for guns which were earlier used for hunting slaves in the hinterland.

Only when the wars of France cease and the Frenchmen come back to that port as before, the slave-trade might pick up and the colony could breathe again.

The situation has been getting worse with capture of two vessels by Frenchmen who had carried away the cargo of ivory, gold, slaves and provisions. This had happened in April and because of that the ships going to the North Province could not take more than just ballast.

The same was likely to happen this year because ivory and gold might not reach in time from the hinterland to leave for the North. [3] This had raised the price of ivory to 132 xerafins per arroba and gold had soared by 37 per cent (?) and even that was not available.

APPENDIX-IV

A Bill of Lading

Vencatesh and Narayan Camotim have handed over to Antonio Jose Pereira in command of vessel Aurora 96 boxes of Malwa opium [4] of *a pico* and half each,[5] to be given to Vitorino Manoel do Loreto, or to Manoel Pereira in his absence, or to Januario Agostinho de Almeida [6] in the absence of either. The ship was taking the opium to Macao. Paid 10 Spanish *patacas* per *pico* as freight fee.

18th April, 1805 ANTONIO MATIAS LOURENCO

APPENDIX-V

Letter from Modi Mervanji Manecgy[7] to Vencatesha and Narayana Camotim.

Bombay, 16th July 1805

Acknowledges receipt of letter of 28th June and thanks for interceding through Major General William Clerk [8] before Duncan on behalf of his son Sapurgy. Asks for a copy of Clerk's letter, which he or his attorney in Bombay, Dadabai, would take to Duncan personally along with his request.

As regards the village has taken note that it can be obtained for 2,000 *xerafins*. The widow, daughter of Manoel Joaquim might give it to him for 1,500 to 1,600 *xerafins*.

Having realized the purchase wants him to keep all the deed papers in order.

Asks the favour of meeting all the expenses without drawing any bill on him for the next four months. Will pay after that with interest. The purchase should be effected by all means.

Claims that Jacinto Domingos from Surat has named Francisco Gomes Loureiro his attorney and is now giving false information about him. Wants a letter of recommendation from the Governor to Gomes Loureiro. If such a letter cannot be obtained, requests the Camotins to write a letter themselves explaining how ungrateful Jacinto had been to him.

APPENDIX-VI

Letter form Domingos Gomes Loureiro[9] & Sons to Vencatesha and Narayana Camotim. Rio de Janeiro, 17th May 1809

The revolution which brought the royal family from Portugual to Brazil, shifting the entire direction of Portuguese commerce had moved them to establish their agency house in Rio. They would take care of any business that the Camotins might entrust them with utmost zeal.

Their ship Rainha dos Anjos is going to visit ports which were closed till then to the businessmen of Brazil. They hoped that the revolution would benefit the business of Asia, and that the goods of Malabar would be especially in demand. Requests all possible assistance for their ship and its super cargo. Simão de Rocha Loureiro and Domingos Alvaro Loureiro.

REFERENCES TO APPENDICES

1. S.P. Sen, *op. cit.*, 189, Couronat was the captain of *Sartine* which brought Saint-Lubin to India. He was thrown into prison by the Marathas on the accusation of Saint-Lubin. Saint-Lubin's mission came to an abrupt end in 1778 with a revolution in Maratha politics and temporary eclipse of Nana Phandnavis.
2. *Ibid.*, 532 ff. Isle de French was the French base when all their possessions in the East were captured by the English. The economy of the island depended on slave-labour.
3. Province of the North included the coastal settlements of the Portuguese between Bombay and Daman.
4. *Cf. supra* no. 43.
5. *Pico* weighed 100 *catties* and was equivalent to 133.3 lb. wt.
6. XCHR: Mhamai House Records — Letter of J.A. Almeida, Macao, 3.12.1805 expressing concern over difficulty of selling the opium of low-quality sent by the Mhamais.
7. Merwanjee Manecgy was a descendant of Rustamgy Manockji who functioned as Portuguese agent at Surat in the late 17th century. From the other correspondence between Merwangy and the Mhamais it can be concluded that the

recommendation sought was aimed at getting the release of a vessel captured by the pirates of Malwan.

8. William Clarke was in command of British occupation forces in Goa during 1799-1815.
9. The Loureiro family owned ships of their own, and several members of the family served as Portuguese factors at Surat. Cf. A.F. Moniz, "A feitoria Portuguesa de Surate", O Oriente Portugues, XV, 1 and 2, 1918, pp. 5-29.

[Reprinted from "Mhamai House Records: Indigenous Sources for Indo-Portuguese Historiography", II *Seminário Internacional de História Indo-Portuguesa: Actas*, ed. Luis de Albuquerque and Inácio Guerreiro, Lisboa, 1985, pp. 931-941].

7

A GOAN OPIUM DEALER WHO ATTEMPTED TO LIBERATE GOA

It is undoubtedly true that nationalist movements or struggles for freedom have been exercises in selfless dedication to a cause on the part of some individuals. However, it would be naïve to believe that the success of such movements and struggles resulted exclusively from the inspiration and drive of such persons. There are always other personal and less noble factors that also play their role and make their contribution. Such private and selfish interests often coincide with the march of the Spirit towards freedom, as Hegel explained metaphysically and he called it "the cunning of reason". However, less metaphysically-inclined minds can also see such sinking of differences with the motivation of reaping a hundredfold after a new dispensation is brought into existence under grateful leaders who could reward the enlightened self-interest.

Any freedom struggle needs to be seen as a web woven with many threads of many hues. Anil Seal's *The Emergence of Indian Nationalism* is one of such welcome approach. [1] There are many other similar and laudable studies as regards the Indian nationalism and struggle for freedom.[2] A cool historical analysis of this nature, exposing the saints and the knaves in Goa's freedom struggle, has not yet been undertaken, and it will not be possible to do so satisfactorily until most of the relevant records, including the archives of the Portuguese military tribunal at Goa, are released for research. Such an analysis is likely to be hazardous also to one who ventures into such a task by inviting the wrath of the knaves, and perhaps of the saints also who may still be around.

Given the reasons and the difficulties for a research undertaking that we consider desirable, the present essay seeks to perform a model exercise on a very modest scale. A theme of Goan history which has found treatment at the macro-level is sought to be projected on a broader canvas in order to draw more than regional interest. "The Bombay Connection" is brought in to shift the focus from local incidents in Goa's liberal-constitutional struggle of the 1820s-30s to extra-regional vested interests.

We start with a quick survey of the existing studies with a two-fold purpose, namely to provide the necessary context and to point out to the shadowy figure of the Bombay Connection looming in the background of the developments taking place in Goa. This is followed up with the shift that we are proposing. Published and new archival evidence are used to unravel the Bombay Connection. It is hoped that this model exercise will encourage younger people to re-write the regional history of Goa with new perspectives and with new evidence.

Goa's Freedom Struggle and the Ghost of Rogerio de Faria

Goan authors of the late 19th century, like Miguel Vicente d'Abreu, J.C. Barreto Miranda, and A.A. Bruto da Costa, have written scholarly works in Portuguese, analysing the political developments of the century with an almost nationalist slant.[3] We need to make concessions to the constraints in which they wrote, and also to their time-bound vision. Still we find in their works much matter that can enable us today to attempt a shift in perspective. A.F. Moniz wrote at the beginning of the 20th century, and he may be classified as a reactionary as compared with the earlier writers, but his *Notícias e Documentos para a História de Damão* contains many pointed references to the "Bombay Connection". They are documents that refer to the administration of the Prefect Bernardo Peres da Silva in Daman (1835-37) and these were published by the author to uphold the honesty of his grandfather, who was an old hand in the Daman administration, but was unceremoniously dismissed and disgraced by the Prefect. Whatever the intentions of the author, he has done excellent service to history by editing many important documents.[4]

The Marquis of Pombal had already utilized the press very skilfully to malign his clerical enemies ("*Os denominados Jesuítas*"), but at the turn of the century the influence of Jacobinism and the Masonic clubs in Portugal saw a flourishing gutter-press that sustained partisan interests. The spill-over of the Portuguese liberalism into Goa brought to Goa a committed official press and much underground pamphleteering. It provides for the historian much material to be critically used.[5] It is stated, for instance, that the first rumblings of the liberal discontent in Goa in 1821 followed the arrival of a copy of the royal decree accepting constitutionalism in Portugal. This copy of the decree was sent to Bernardo Peres da Silva by Rogerio de Faria from Bombay.[6] The liberal coup on 16th September 1821 deposed the Viceroy Count of Rio Pardo and established a Junta rule. It was the beginning of a long political turmoil, reflecting the instability that reigned in Portugal. The Goans were growing in political maturity, and they could see more and more clearly that all the noise and liberal proclamations by the Portuguese and the white settlers of Goa did not coincide with their native self-respect and their desire for self-rule. There were, of course, a few enlightened white sympathisers. Among these stood out boldly the friar-archbishop of Goa, D. Manoel de S. Galdino. For voicing boldly the discontended feelings of the local people against the oppressive rule of the Junta and its white supporters, this spiritual leader was forced to shift his residence to Sunkery, across the southern border of Goa. We know from a few published extracts of the archbishop's correspondence, intercepted by this political enemies, that he was in contact with Rogerio de Faria of Bombay.[7]

The liberal-constitutional regime had given the Goans the opportunity of sending their elected representatives to the House of Representatives in Portugal. The system actually favoured the Portuguese-educated landed gentry, but one could still notice wide popular support for the elected representatives. This was obviously generated by the peoples' anti-colonial feelings that had no other viable outlet. In spite of the efforts of the white settlers to manoeuvre the elections with their political power and military intimidation, they could find no popular support for their candidates. Bernardo Peres da Silva, a Goan and trained in medicine, was elected in every election held from 1822 till 1842. Once, in 1836, when he was in exile (to which we shall turn our attention soon) the Portuguese forced an election in which only two European-controlled constituencies participated, while the remaining four stayed away.[8]

Bernardo Peres da Silva had fought actively on the side of the liberals in Portugal. His son, serving in the military in Portugal, had also been actively involved in defending the cause of Prince Regent Pedro, and was in the expeditionary force that landed in Portugal from Terceira and won a decisive victory for the liberals in 1834. It was then that Prince Pedro appointed Bernardo Peres da Silva Prefect of the Portuguese State of India.[9] It was a new designation for viceroy or governor of earlier times. The arrival of the Prefect in Goa on 10th January 1835 created panic and anxiety among the beneficiaries of the erstwhile regime. The administrative changes and fresh appointments in the Departments of Justice and Finance, undertaken by the Prefect within a week of taking office, led to a coup by the old guard and the Prefect was forced to leave Goa on 1st February, that is, just after a fortnight in power. His many native supporters and some white sympathisers could do nothing against the military opposition to protect the Prefect. They were themselves soon forced to seek security outside Goa, along the coast from Malvan to Daman. It should be noticed that the administration in Daman and Diu remained loyal to the Prefect as the legitimate authority until a substitute was officially sent from Portugal in 1837.[10]

Bernardo Peres da Silva was solemnly received in Daman in July 1835. Till then, for nearly five months after his deposition, he was in Bombay. He spent those months preparing an expeditionary force to recapture Goa by force. Perhaps the memory of the expeditionary force that gained Portugal for the liberals in 1834 was the source of inspiration for his plans. The undertaking had the active support of Rogerio de Faria, who was also hosting the Prefect in Bombay. The papers in Bombay were reporting the progress of the plans. For instance, *The Bombay Courier* of 26th May 1835 describes the composition of the expeditionary crew: "Sr. Peres it seems is determined to follow the example of Don Pedro in this country, and for this purpose has collected out of the Bazar a body of nearly three hundred as ragged-looking fellows as ever were seen". The reporter continues: "The quantity of opium smuggled this year into Damaun, over the revenues of which he possesses some control, having been much greater than usual, unexpected resources were placed at his disposal, and everything has since gone smoothly up to the present moment". He concludes: "It only remains to be seen whether fortune will continue to smile and as a few days will now settle this momentous question, we shall not venture to hazard an opinion regarding it".[11]

The liberals do not seem to have learned from the repeated mistakes of the old regime in matters of Portuguese shipping. Late departures and consequent running into stormy weather had caused greater damage to Portuguese shipping since they arrived in the East than did the Dutch or the pirates.[12] The expeditionary force of the Prefect had left Bombay on 27th May, disregarding public warnings of the advancing monsoon that had set in since some days at Cochin. Right enough, the expeditionary fleet that had embarked in two lumber-boats converted into gun-boats, a ketch and a corvette, was wrecked by a thunderstorm and was back in Bombay on the fifth day in a wretched condition and with heavy casualties. The *Bombay Courier* had the following editorial comment on 6th June 1835 : "The Portuguese corvette with Sr. Peres, returned yesterday, after an unavailing attempt to contend against the southwest monsoon, which appears to have been totally forgotten in fitting out the expedition against Goa. The rest of the small craft which accompanied her arrived here a day or two previously, and are now scattered about the harbour in a disabled state. Thus, we presume, a stop has been put to the efforts against Goa for some months at least, if not for ever. What will become of the motley crowd of Sindians, Cutchees, Moghuls and people without any designation whatever, who composed the expedition remains to be seen. But come what may, we trust for the security of private property that measures will be adopted to prevent them from congregating in Bombay". I have not followed the worries of the Bombayites, but the Prefect had left Bombay and entrenched himself in Daman as we have already mentioned earlier. Once there, the son-in-law and partner of Sir Rogerio de Faria submitted a bill for Rs. 67,957 to the Prefect. It was meant to recover expenditure on arms supplied for the defence of Daman and Diu, as well as the expenses of the expedition that had failed.[13]

The Bombay Connection into Focus: Rogerio de Faria and CIA

All the above sources of information do not take us further than we have reached in knowing the activities or the personality of Rogerio de Faria. We are left with the impression that he was a silent operator. The CIA after his name has nothing to do with the modern equivalent of it. It was the Portuguese abbreviation for Company because he had registered himself as a Portuguese national domiciled in Bombay.

My interest in Rogerio de Faria was aroused when a part of his business correspondence, dating from 1789 to 1830, with the Mhamai Kamat Agency House in Goa came into my hands a couple of years ago. This correspondence includes business reports, balance-sheets, lading-bills, bills of exchange, receipts, and even mere friendly letters. Surprisingly, there is no reference in this correspondence to the political development in Goa. This may be explained by the fact that this correspondence is reduced to a trickle after 1871. Whatever correspondence followed was more to seek closure of acounts, because in 1818 the Mhamai House was charged with heavy indebtedness to the State

Exchequer in connnection with tax-farming and it nearly declared itself insolvent.[14] The papers prior to 1818 contain much interesting information that can help us to correct and supplement whatever we know about Rogerio de Faria from a few contemporary published sources and from a few late and sketchy biographies.

The earliest published reference to Rogerio de Faria occurs in Lady West's *Journal.* Sir Edward West, the Chief Justice of the Supreme Court of judicature of the Bombay Presidency, and his wife had been on a visit to Goa from 7th to 23rd December 1824. It appears from the correspondence of Rogerio de Faria that he was instrumental in making arrangements for their stay in Goa through the agency of the Mhamai House.[15] However, Lady West's *Journal* has no mention of de Faria in this connection. She has two interesting entries on him though: "Sir Roger de Taria (sic) has sent me 2 sheep and a keg of humps, tongues, and so on. As he is a great Portuguese merchant I thought I could not refuse all, and therefore, accepted of the dead stock (Sept. 12, 1825)", and "Even Portuguese Merchants are not to be depended upon, for yesterday a Cause came on in Court in which Sir Roger de Taria (sic) was interested. It taught me not to put any trust in man" (Sept. 13, 1825).[16]

The only other contemporary published account of Sir Rogerio is found in Abbé Cottineau's Journal. Cottineau had been to his house, which he describes as "commanding a most lovely view of the sea, the ramparts, the suburbs, the city, the Colaba island, and the West coast as far as the so-called Malabar Point". He also recounts that Sir Rogerio's old father was fairer than the son, who was then a widower with one son and eight daughters. Cottineau had dined with the family, and he tells us that after dinner Sir Rogerio smoked a pipe in the Indian fashion whose reed passed through a cooler.[17] This small concluding detail tends to suggest that Rogerio was smoking opium. It was in opium-peddling that he made his fortune. He was one of those in country trade which changed the face of Bombay in the first half of the 19th century . It is unfortunate that Gillian Tindall's very recent study of the growth of Bombay has only the Parsee community in focus and the Indo-Portuguese have been dismissed with a passing comment amounting to a taunt: "They are known for their sallow countenance, slovenly gait, and mimicry of the European fashions".[18]

It is not sufficiently known that there were several small Indo-Portuguese firms that tried their luck in the commercial world of nineteenth century rising Bombay. Most of them were small-fry and did not survive beyond the first quarter of the century, when the mortality among the small firms proved to be very high. Following the end of Company's monopoly in 1813 the process of survival of the fittest among the participants in the country trade had begun.[19] The history of many of those little concerns that were wiped out will never be sufficiently known, and that deprives us of details which alone could complete the picture of the rise of the Indian business world.

We are not able to fully corroborate the statement, but we are told by the otherwise critical Indo-Portuguese administrator-historian, J.H. da Cunha-Rivara, that Sir Jamshetjee Jeejeebhoy, the most glamorous Parsee figure of the mid-nineteenth century in the annals of Bombay, started his prosperous career as a simple clerk in the firm of Rogerio de Faria. [20] Reporting the death of Sir Rogerio's daughter, Miss Margaret de Faria, the *Bombay Gazette* of 7 October, 1889 added that Sir Jamsethjee had made his first voyage to China in a ship belonging to Sir Rogerio de Faria. A short, but informative life account of Sir Rogerio in Gujarati was published in 1835 as a result of a loan given to a Governor of Goa, and which led to Sir Rogerio's bankruptcy in December 1838. The author concludes that Sir Rogerio had no one to look after him during the sunset of his life, and that Sir Jamsethjee assisted him while he was alive and provided a bungalow and regular living allowance to his descendants in perpetuity.[21] This seems to be confirmed by what Sir Jamsethjee was writing on 26 November 1838 to his correspondent William Jardine in Canton:

> "You will be sorry to hear poor Sir Roger de Faria delivered his affairs to the Court, his assets apparently 50 per cent which will keep out from going to jail-my good friend... I have some regard to his family and cannot help of avoiding this large number of persons to provide with."[22]

For nearly half a century, till the financial disaster overtook him in 1838, Rogerio de Faria had been riding quite high on the crest of the opium wave. When the Macau route was the only legitimate exception to the Canton system, he had claimed the right on the basis of his Portuguese nationality to enjoy the privileges of the Macau residents in the China trade in spite of much resentment and resistance of the local interests. With his base at Bengal, he had opened a branch house in Macau in 1798.[23] Due to the deteriorating health of his father who was assisting him in Bengal during his business trips to Macau and Canton, he shifted his base to Bombay around 1803.[24] He had kept up his contacts with the State authorities in Goa, and opened trade contacts with Brazil in the wake of the shift of the Portuguese royal seat to that country following the occupation of Portugal by the Nepoleonic forces. When his ship entered Rio for the first time, it brought him an award of knighthood from the King. Apparently, he had little regard for honours that did not bring financial benefits along. Writing to the Mhamais in November 1811, he complains about getting an honour with no exemption in customs duties to maintain such an honour.[25]

The award of knighthood did earn for him the title of *Sir* in the Bombay circles. He was also appointed Director of the Portuguese counter at Surat for three years from 1826. [26] He exploited his standing with the Portuguese authorities to the full to promote his business interests. From 1820s he had joined the country traders who were shipping opium directly to Lintin, by-passing the claims of Macau. He had also the most advantageous position among the country traders, because his standing with the authorities in Daman gave him a near-monopoly control of the East India Company. Two-thirds of Malwa was carried by the circuitous route of Daman, and only one-third via Bombay until the Company decided to combat this last challenge to its monopoly controls and introduced 'transit passes' in Bombay in 1831. As a result, nine-tenths of Malwa began moving out via Bombay.[27]

It is obvious from the above that the noose was tightening, and the end of Rogerio de Faria and CIA was drawing near. His involvement in the Goa affairs and the problems of the Prefect may be explained as sentimental as well as a business calculation. He had raised loans to meet the expenses of the expeditionary force and had issued bills in favour of Sir Jamsethjee of Bombay and Motichund in Ahmedabad. The bills were to be paid by the Prefect on taking charge of the Daman administration in cash or through exemptions of customs duties. Apparently, the Prefect failed to keep his word, because the bureaucracy of Daman that had upheld his legitimacy boldly, was equally bold in questioning the legality of his procedures for clearing the debts.[28]

By failing to honour the bills after repeated reminders of the creditors, Rogerio de Faria lost his credibility in the business world, and that was the last thing he could afford. Sir Jamsethjee had sounded a warning to this effect in a letter he addressed to him on 29th July, 1835 : *You seem to be quite ignorant of what the result will be in the end (emphasis added).* Had it been known to the Marwadies that the Bill granted to Motichund and me was dishonoured after its being put off from day to day for so long a time, I am sure that both the Marwadies and Ahmedabad merchants would always willingly follow Motichund's advice. You are perfectly aware of Motichund's influence over them. (...) In conclusion I have only to add that if they do not choose to pass the Bills in payment of the duty or pay the amount in cash the Bills must be protested for non-payment and we must make our agents to send back to Bombay as they are afraid to do anything of this sort. I trust you will write to Daman confidentially and see that the matter is arranged without delay as we must hold you responsible.[29]

Conclusion

It is not important for us to conclude with the very end of Rogerio de Faria's misfortunes. After losing his financial world, he also lost his only son a couple of years before he died in 1848. Both the losses were beyond his control. His son died of tetanus after an accidental fall. [30] His financial strangulation may be regarded also as unavoidable, while his bungling in Goa's freedom struggle provided only an occasion that accelerated the pace of the fall.

REFERENCES AND NOTES

1. A. Seal, *The Emergence of Indian Nationalism: Competition and Collaboration in the Later Nineteenth Century*, Cambridge, 1968.
2. The works of Bipin Chandra, J.C. Masselos, Amles Tripathi, A.R. Desai, Leonard A. Gordon, Dietmar Rothermund, Gordon Johnson, Christine Dobbin may be usefully consulted for their analyses of Indian nationalism.
3. M.V. de Abreu, *Relação das Alterações Políticas de Goa desde 16 de Setembro de 1821 a 18 de Outubro de 1822*, Panjim, 1862; A.A. Bruto da Costa, *As Revoluções Políticas da India Portuguesa do Século XIX*, Margão, 1896; J.V. Barreto de Miranda, *Quadros históricos de Goa*, Margão, 1863-1865.
4. A.F. Moniz, *Notícias e Documentos para a História de Damão*, Bastora, 1900-17. 4 vols. Documentation relevant for the present essay are found in vols. 2 & 4.
5. J. N. da Fonseca, *An Historical and Archaeological Sketch of the City of Goa*, Bombay, 1878, pp. 59-61. Cf. H.V. Livermore, *A New History of Portugal*, London, 1967, p. 264.
6. Costa, *op. cit.*, p. 14.
7. *Ibid.*. p. 42.
8. M.V. de Abreu, *Noção de Alguns Filhos Distintos da India Portuguesa*, Panjim, 1874, p. 53.
9. M.V. de Abreu, *Relação*, p. 36.
10. Moniz, *op. cit.*, IV, pp. 121ff.
11. *The Bombay Courier* editorials were quite critical of the Prefect and his plans.

This attitude invited many letters from the part of the Prefect and are published in the bi-weekly. The controversy is enlightening.

12. C.R. Boxer, *Portuguese India in the Mid-Seventeenth Century,* Delhi, 1980, pp. 23ff.
13. Moniz, *op. cit.,* IV, p. 125.
14. T. R. de Souza, "Mhamai House Records: Indigenous Sources for Indo-Portuguese Historiography", *The Indian Archives,* XXXI, no. 1, Jan-June 1982, pp. 25-45.
15. Ms. in the author's collection. It is a letter of Rogerio de Faria, dated 30 November 1823.
16. F. D. Drewitt, *Bombay in the Days of George IV: Memoirs of Sir Edward West,* London, 1907, p. 185.
17. *Instituto Vasco da Gama,* May, 1874, no. 29, p. 105.
18. G. Tindall, *City of Gold,* London, 1982, pp. 182-183.
19. M. Greenberg, *British Trade and the Opening of China 1800-1842,* New York, 1951, pp. 51ff.
20. J.H. da Cunha Rivara, "Jornadas as praças do norte em 1859", *Instituto Vasco da Gama,* Panjim, 1872, p. 189.
21. R.F. Wachha, *Mumbayno Bahar,* I, Bombay, 1874, pp. 235-237.
22. Sir J.J. Papers (University of Bombay): no. 358, p. 213.
23. Historical Archives of Goa (HAG): Ms. 1296, *Correspondência de Macau,* fls.74, 281.
24. Ms. in author's collection. Letters of Rogerio de Faria, dated 5-8-1803, and 22-1-1816.
25. Ms. in author's collection. Letter of Rogerio de Faria, dated 10-11-1811.
26. A.F. Moniz, "A Feitoria Portuguesa de Surrate", *O Oriente Portugues,* XXV (1918), n. 1 & 2, p. 27.
27. Greenberg, *op. cit.,* p. 124 ff.
28. Moniz, *Notícias e Documentos para a História de Damão,* IV, pp. 178 ff.
29. Sir J.J. Papers (University of Bombay): no. 351, fls. 169v-171v.
30. A.M. da Cunha, *Sir Roger de Faria,* Panjim, 1928: 12. This little booklet of 30p. gives more details about the numerous progeny of Sir Roger than about him. The author fits distantly in one of the lines, and the work seems to have been undertaken to trace this link.

[Reprinted from *Indo-Portuguese History Old Issues,* New Questions, ed. Teotonio R. de Souza, New Delhi, 1985, pp. 101-113.]

8

ROGERIO DE FARIA'S CHINA LINKS

I have introduced Rogerio de Faria and his role in an aborted plan aimed at restoring to power his friend Bernardo Peres da Silva who had been ousted by the Goan mestiço-dominated military from his job as *Prefeito* of the *Estado da India*. Faria's business calculations failed narrowly because of a pre-monsoon storm which dashed the expeditionary fleet of his mercenaries against rocks, off Vingurla coast at the end of May 1835.[1]

I wish to reconstruct here his links with China as a "country trader". The information available is fragmentary, but it enables us to add a little more to our knowledge of the "country trade" scenario that forms an important phase of the history of the establishment of the British control over the trade in the Indian Ocean and the British imperial control over India. The private papers of Rogerio de Faria which I obtained from the Mhamay family along with other surviving family business papers, help us to have a glimpse into the role, however limited, though not insignificant, played by the losers in the game, such as the various free traders and agency houses that in the first three decades of the 19th century dominated Bombay based "country trade". Miguel de Lima e Souza was one of the Indo-Portuguese businessmen who has received much attention as having guided the policies of Jonathan Duncan in Gujarat, as Murdoch Brown did in Malabar.[2]

Surprisingly there is very little information in this correspondence about Faria's involvement in opium trade. Writing from Bombay on 26th February, 1817, Faria informed Mhamai Brothers that a Bania from Daman had built a vessel (*palla*) for his brother-in-law based in Bombay. Antonio Pereira and some other Banias of Bombay wanted to take that vessel for freight to Macau. Faria wants Mhamai Brothers not to assist that group, but to back his own friend Vicente Salvador

Rodrigues (Judge at Daman, formerly at Macau!) who wanted to take on hire a vessel named *Principe Regente*, just manufactured in Daman and belonging to Manuel Pereira, Rogerio's friend from Macau, to send opium and cotton to China.[3] However, Faria was not just helping others as it may appear from this reference. He was closely and personally involved in the China trade, particularly its opium trade, from the very early beginnings of that trade. Greenberg mentions Sir Roger Faria only passingly as an *Anglicised Portuguese of Bombay* who along with some others interested in opium trade in the Portuguese jurisdiction and allied with Magniac & Co. thwarted the attempt made by James Matheson and Jardine to ship Malwa opium directly from the West coast of India. Faria is mentioned as having bribed successfully the Judge of Daman to keep these other interests out.[4] In a more recent study Gervase ClarenceSmith tells us that the Portuguese derived only modest benefits form this infamous commerce, and identifies the private traders as a motley collection of Scots, British Indians, Armenians and others, and *the only notable Portuguese among them was Rogerio de Faria.*[5]

Contrary to this picture, which is supported by archival information elsewhere, Mhamai House Papers include just two letters written by Faria from Pulo Pinao on 25th and 29th June 1798, an incomplete (only last page surviving) letter written from Macau on 28 August, 1978, and two letters written from Canton in 1799 and 1800. It is a strange coincidence that Jardine Matheson ledgers that survive also begin in 1799.[6] On 31 December, 1799 Faria sent a letter with a friend, a Muslim Nacoda, named Mohamed Ibrahim, who had stayed in Canton for three years. He had asked this friend to arrange some goods from Goa through the agency of Mhamai House. He wants them to send the goods by the Macau ship *Flor de Mar*. Faria promises to take care of the payment of costs to Mhamais through the same Nacoda in Bombay. He refers in the same letter to a surgeon and to one Cordeiro deported to Timor. They had escaped from Macau and were caught in Canton and were being sent back to Macau.[7] In the only other letter written from Canton about a year later on 20 November, 1800, Faria acknowledges the letters sent to him by the Mhamai Brothers through Senhor D. Antonio d'Eça, and then informs the brothers that he is due to leave for Bengal before next monsoon as instructed by his father. And adds: " I am not sure if I will return to China, but I am glad I have fulfilled my desire of establishing business houses and contacts in Macau, and even though the municipal councillors there were opposed to me initially, they have turned into my friends and admirers". He refers to various individuals in Goa whose business interests he looked after in China. Among them were Panduranga and Vasudeva Sinay Cabady, Vitogy and Narba Naik Corondo, Roullu Naik, Govinda and Ram Custa Sinay. Mhamay Brothers seem to have ordered some Chinese tea-pots, which Faria had arranged to be sent from Macau through Carlos Jose Pereira.[8]

The Governor General in Goa, Francisco Antonio da Veiga Cabral issued a licence to Rogerio de Faria, who is referred to as native of Chorão island of Goa (*sic*) to establish a business house in Macau. He also ordered the Municipality of Macau to issue a safe conduct to Faria for a ship which he was in the process of acquiring as soon as his business house was set up. This was communicated by the Goa authorities to the Captain General of Macau D. Cristovão Pereira de Castro on 7 May 1798.[9]

The above-mentioned licence was issued on 2nd May and it entitled Faria to trade in all types of goods as allowed to other subjects of the Portuguese crown and subject to payment of dues to the Customs as per rules. He was to be allowed to run his own ship to transport personal goods and those of others to Goa and to any ports of Asia with safe conduct issued by the Municipality of Macau.[10]

The Captain General of Macau acknowledged on 15th May the instructions of Goa authorities and informed them about the arrival of Faria and his moves to set up a business house in partnership with Manuel de Souza. He further informed that Faria had left for Canton and was still there attending to his business.[11]

It is clear from the references to Vincente Salvador Rodrigues, Manuel Pereira and to D. Antonio d'Eça in the few letters of Faria quoted above that he had managed to win friends among the Macau officialdom who could clear the way for his business interests in Macau. Possibly, as we shall see, these connections may have also drawn Faria into the local rivalry. Manuel Pereira figures among the *vereadores* in 1799 and among the *juizes* in 1801, while D. Antonio d'Eça was a *juiz* of the *Senado* in 1800.[12]

Faria was telling the truth in the letter written to Mhamai Brothers and quoted above, concerning the initial resistance to his plans on the part of the municipal council of Macau. We read in a letter addressed by the Board of the said Council on 22 December, 1798 that they have reservations about obeying the instructions issued by the Goa authorities and endorsed by the Captain General and Governor of Macau. They refer to a letter they had written two years back with reference to *chalupa* Carmo and the introduction of opium into Macau by Rogerio de Faria. They repeat now that "this man is likely to bring about a visible ruin to the city of Macau with the establishment of his business in it. The councillors claim that they are *not moved by any spirit of intrigue, but only by their concern for the commonweal of the city*".[13] The ship *Carmo* belonging to Francisco Joze de Paiva had arrived from Bengal with 441 chests of opium sent by Faria. The consignment was held in Macau Customs till the inquiry was held to establish the right to introduce such a commodity by a non-Portuguese and non-residents of Macau. The goods were released after Faria obtained a sentence in his favour. Until then only the "great house of Barretos" (*grande caza dos Barretos*) was referred to as Portuguese.[14] The Macau municipality continued to press the Government authorities to restrict the opium trading rights in Macau only to the Portuguese married settlers (*Portugueses cazados*) of Macau.[15] In a memorandum sent by the Bishop of Macau, he too cautioned against opening exceptions to the prevailing rules that restricted the opium trade to the residents of Macau. He refers to Rogerio de Faria, *que sendo naturalizado em Bengala se fez Portuguez,* and warns that such violations of the tradition would leave the doors wide open to foreigners to introduce any amount of opium they may like into Macau.[16]

Rogerio de Faria's father, João de Faria, had started a business house in Calcutta, initially known as Bruce, Faria & Co. Faria family hailed from St. Ines in Goa, and Rogerio was married to a lady from Sirula. He retained great love for Goa all through his life. He paid regular visits to Goa for relaxation, and always refers to Goa in his correspondence with the Mhamais as *minha pátria*. Possibly he was also under the spell of a dancing girl from the folkloric Shiroda. The collection of papers pertaining to Rogerio contains receipts of regular monthly payments of 30 *xerafins* to *bailadeira* Ba. It is possible also that Faria was only acting as a channel for remmittance of money from Bengal to Goa by a son of this dancing girl. The name of the son is mentioned as Francisco de Souza and he lived somewhere in Bengal. There are receipts of other such remittances arranged by Faria through the mediation of Mhamai Brothers to different parties in Goa with relatives in Bengal.

Even though Faria had expressed his uncertainty about returning to China in his letter of December 1800, we know it from his later correspondence that he had been back to Canton and was there till January 1803. Apparently it was becoming difficult for the private merchants to beat the growing control of the Honourable East India

Company not only over the sale of opium in Bengal, but even over its production there since 1797. That is when the Malwa opium started growing in popularity among the country traders, and Rogerio de Faria seems to have made up his mind to shift his base of operations closer to his *patria*. He came to Bombay in May of 1803 and informed the Mhamai Brothers of his intentions to make the shift permanent. Poor health of his father is quoted as a reason, though his father continued to operate from Bengal for at least two more decades and came to Bombay only a few years before his death in May 1828 at a ripe age of 80.[17]

Rogerio de Faria established himself very well in Bombay and was listed in the Directories and Almanacs of Bombay as "Portuguese Merchant and Agency House of Sir Roger de Faria and Co." . He kept up his contacts with the State authorities in Goa, and opened trade contacts with Brazil in the wake of the shift of the Portuguese royal seat to that country following the occupation of Portugal by the Napoleonic forces. When Faria's ship (*gallera*) *Grão Cruz de Aviz* entered Rio for the first time, it brought for Faria the award of knighthood from the royal court. However, Faria was writing to Mhamai Brothers on 10 November, 1811 that he would appreciate the award more if it was accompanied by some exemption in customs duties which would enable him to sustain the dignity of knighthood conferred on him! [18] The knighthood earned him the title of Sir in the Bombay society. He was later appointed Director of the Portuguese factory at Surat for a period of three years from 1826 and also looked after the Portuguese commercial interests in Bombay.[19] These official positions only enhanced the standing which Faria already had as a Portuguese merchant with trade links with Macau, Brazil, Daman and Surat. Faria's correspondence with the Mhamays has frequent references to his visits and contacts with Daman and Surat much before he is appointed Portuguese factor of Surat. He was taking advantage of the revival of the direct Portuguese trade from Brazil with India in the cloths of Daman and Surat. The Portuguese traders made hay when the English and French were going for each other.[20] The British ban on exports of opium from Bombay and the restrictions in Macau to importing opium only in Portuguese-flagged ships had made Daman a bustling exit point for the Malwa opium exporters.[21] Rogerio de Faria had limited stakes in the Brazil trade and with the end of the Napoleonic wars the earlier brighter prospects had waned, but he became increasingly involved in the opium trading and had a lion's share in it.

Opium trade statistics need to be taken as only partially indicative of the real situation. Rogerio de Faria had at least four ships of his own, named *Grão Cruz de Aviz, Gloriozo* (later named *D. Manoel de Portugal*), *Margaret Crawford, Boa Esperança*, which operated on different routes. Faria was also frequently sending his cargo on other vessels like *Rainha dos Anjos* and *Robusto* to Brazil and Portugal; *Cidade de Damão, Carmo, Principe Regente, Leal Portugues, Angelica, Pascoa, Rozalia, Caçador, Bons Amigos, Rozario, Thereza,* etc. owned by Indo-Portuguese businessmen plied between Moçambique, Daman, Goa, Bengal and China. On this eastern route he often sought freight space on vessels owned by private English traders as well. Faria also preferred English supercargos for his ships and some accommodating Portuguese as second-in-command. Besides taking care of eventual political-diplomatic conflicts by such an arrangement, he had great regard for what he refers to in his correspondence as the disciplined and responsible behaviour of the English pilots and supercargos compared with others.[22]

One needs to only go through the long series of volumes in Goa Historical Archives pertaining to Daman and Macau, the series of *Alfandegas de Goa*, and the *Monções do Reino* correspondence (particularly Ms 205-B) to get a somewhat detailed picture of the opium trade between Portuguesc western India and China. A fully complete picture will be as good as anyone's guess. From what I have been able to tally after a very rapid survey of these sources Faria had dispatched over 350 chests of opium during 1796-1801 from Bengal, and from 1816 to 1819 he paid 37847 taels as customs duty for opium he sent to Macau from western India. The customs duty in Daman was originally 4%, later reduced to 2.5%. From this once could conclude the actual value of the shipments of opium by Faria during 1816-1819. Only from 1825 to 1828 he sent opium worth Rs. 12,61,972 to Lentin on the account of various residents of Macau, chiefly to Paiva & Sons and Albino G. de Araujo. Moniz has given the figures of opium exports from Daman in 1823 in a single ship and mentioned as the first consignment to leave directly from Daman. Rogerio de Faria topped the list with 537 chests worth Rs. 6,15,420.[23] Even though the Macau officialdom protested strongly against the bypassing of Macau by those exporting opium from western India to Lintin, as revealed by the above information many business partners of Faria were *Macaenses* themselves bypassing the official interests of Macau. Only men like Faria became an obvious target of their protests and accusations of being unpatriotic. It was not because the Macaenses were more patriotic, but because they were not doing as well as the Bombay merchants with closer links with Daman in 1820s, that is when Daman was handling nearly 2/3 of the the opium exports from western India.[24] Macau authorities tried even to intercept and hold a vessel of Faria despite a passport it carried allowing it to go straight to Lentin in July 1828. Only after keeping guarantee money for payment of unloading duties the ship was released. On complaints of Faria the Goa authorities issued an order to Macau on 12 January 1829 to refund the amount charged.[25] Macau also tried to impose a ban on residence of any foreign merchants in Macau, to which England responded by questioning the Portuguese sovereignty over Macau. The Portuguese had to back down and withdraw the legislation and claims it embodied.[26]

I shall not repeat here what is known about the measures adopted by the British to gain control over the opium trade and squeezing out the agency houses and private merchants who dominated the scene during the first three decades of the 19th century. The defeat of the Marathas and the control over the Mughal administration enabled the British to gradually enforce agreements upon the native princes for restricting cultivation of Malwa opium. The Portuguese outlet was challenged by introducing transit passes at Bombay from 1831 at increasingly more competitive rate, thereby making the smuggling through Daman unprofitable. Many small firms had already gone out of business earlier, and the "cotton slum" became more critical in 20s, caused earlier by scarcity of funds channeled to England for safety during wars in Europe, but also and largely by over-competition and over-supply, as well as by shift to investment in opium. Faria's correspondence has frequent references to this slump and to scarcity of easy finance. He refers to the collapse of some of his business friends, including his close associate Joze Francisco Pereira & Co., and comments about their reckless management of funds (*grandes cavalarias*).[27] But the growing control over smuggling of opium was tightening the noose round Faria's neck. With the arrival of faster clippers and better credit facilities available to the English traders at home and in the empire overseas made the old ships a liability for most country traders, and possibly for Faria as well. His apparent miscalculation and sentimental investment of funds in a political adventure in Goa in 1835 may have been a last ditch effort of Faria to fight against the tide. He hoped to hold the administration of Daman at ransom under the pretext of organizing a force that would ensure the defence of Daman and Diu against any attempt by the military in Goa that had ousted Bernardo Peres da Silva who had found welcome in Daman. Military supplies to the Prefect was a good alibi to lend amounts that could hardly be checked. Faria's brother-in-law Francisco

Antonio de Carvalho was put in charge of the project. The amount was to be repaid through exemption of customs duty at Daman. However, the events turned out differently and Faria defaulted on some deals with some Marwadis on the basis of mortgage and repayment through Daman customs. This eventually led to his declaring bankruptcy in December 1838. It only hastened his downfall that was already on the cards. Of the cargoes of opium surrendered to the Chinese in 1839 the largest amount belonged to Indian merchants of Bombay, and Faria would certainly be among the losers if he had not lost already![28] That was the end of Faria's nearly 40 years of links with China.

REFERENCES AND NOTES

1. Teotonio R. de Souza, ed. *Indo-Portuguese History: Old Issues*, New Questions, New Delhi, 1985, 102-113.
2. Both these advisers are studied in quite some detail by Pamela Nightingale in *Trade and Empire in Western India, 1787-1806* (Cambridge, 1970). Both men are shown as pursuing their own private interests under the guise of serving the interests of the East India Company. Incidentally, Mhamai House Papers include correspondence with Murdoch Brown and I have already presented the nature of its contents in a study of "Goa-Mahe Trade Links", *Studies in Maritime History*, ed. K.S. Mathew, Pondicherry, 1990, pp. 165-174.
3. XCHR: Mhamai House Papers.
4. Michael Greenberg, *British Trade and the Opening of China, 1800-1842)*, New York, 1979 (Reprint of 1951 Cambridge edition), p. 125.
5. Gervase Clarence-Smith, The *Third Portuguese Empire*, Manchester, 1985, p. 26.
6. Michael Greenberg, *op. cit.*, p. 28.
7. XCHR: Mhamai House Papers.
8. XCHR: Mhamai House Papers.
9. HAG: Ms 1296, fl. 10.
10. *Ibid.*, fl. 74.
11. *Ibid.*, fl. 213; XCHR: Mhamai House Papers — Rogerio de Faria's letter from Pulo Pinao to Felix Joze Coimbra his representative in Macau. Refers also to a letter he is sending to be handed over to Manuel de Souza.
12. *Ibid.*, fls. 150-153.
13. *Ibid.*, fl. 251.
14. HAG: Ms 1295,, fl. 77v. Joze Barreto & Sons were acting as attorneys and agents of Faria in Bengal after he shifted to Bombay. Cf. HAG: Mhamai House Papers, Faria's letter of 10-9-1814.
15. *Ibid.*, fls. 77, 139.
16. *Ibid.*, fls. 148-153.
17. XCHR: Mhamai House Papers — Faria's letter dtd. 5-8-1803; Antonio Maria da Cunha, *Sir Roger de Faria: Notas Genealógicas e Biográficas*, Nova Goa, 1928, pp. 3-4.

18. XCHR: Mhamai House Papers — Faria's letter dated 7 July 1810 informs Mhamays about the purchase of *Grão Cruz de Aviz* from Vincente Luis and Agostinho de Souza from Daman. He wanted Mhamays to arrange Balghat cloths of different varieties worth Rs. 15-16,000 offering one-third of the cost in advance and a commission of 1/2% in addition to 2%. In a letter dated 10-11-1811 he acknowledges the receipt of a letter from the Chief Secretary of Goa Government including a copy of the award of the Habit of Christ.
19. A. F. Moniz, "A Feitoria Portuguesa de Surrate", *O Oriente Portugues*, XXV (1918), nn. 1 & 2, p. 27; HAG: *Monções do Reino*. Ms. 211, fl. 326.
20. M.N. Pearson, "Goa-based seaborne trade: 17th-18th centuries", *Goa Through the Ages*, II, ed. Teotonio R. de Souza, New Delhi, 1990, p. 171.
21. Celsa Pinto, "Goa-based overseas and coastal trade: 18th and 19th centuries", *Goa Through the Ages*, II, pp. 181-186.
22. XCHR: Mhamai House Papers — Faria's letter of 27-8-1811.
23. Celsa Pinto, *op. cit.;* HAG: Mss. 1063 ff. (on Daman), Mss 1315-1342 (on Macau) to mention only those which I had time to consult hurriedly with the help of a list of references given to me by Rudy Bauss in March 1981. I am grateful to him for bringing this material to my notice. Celsa Pinto has discussed this subject in greater detail in her doctoral dissertation under my guidance. Her thesis approved by the Goa University is due to appear in print very soon. *Cf.* A.F. Moniz, *Notícias e Documentos para a história de Damão*, II, Bastorá, 1904, pp. 174-176.
24. Bombay Archives: Mss Revenue Department, no. 79/1823, fls. 41v-43v.
25. HAG: Macau — Ms 1327, fls. 339-340; *Monções do Reino* — Ms 203-B, docs. dated 22 July 1828, and 31 Jan. 1829.
26. HAG: Macau— Ms. 1334, fl. 77v, *Monções do Reino* Ms 200-A, fls. 298-298v; Greeberg, op.cit., 134-135.
27. XCHR: Mhamai House Papers — Faria's letters dated 8-4- 1813, 26-6-1813. Warns Mhamai Brothers about their growing balance of payments on his accounts, and threatens them about over-drafts.
28. A. F. Moniz, *op. cit.*, IV, Bastorá, 1917, pp. 178-193; Bombay University: Mss. Jamsetjee Jejeebhoy Papers, No. 351, fls. 169v-171v: Informing William Jardine in Canton about the sorry plight of Sir Roger de Faria in his letter dated 26 November 1838. Asiya Siddiqi, "The business world of Jamsetjee Jejeebhoy", *The Indian Economic and Social History Review*, XIX, nos. 3 & 4, pp. 301-324.

[This is an updated version of "Rogerio de Faria: An Indo-Portuguese Trader with China Links", *Actas do VI Seminário Internacional de História Indo-Portuguesa*, ed. Artur Teodoro de Matos e L. F. e Reis Thomaz, Macau, 1993, pp. 309-319.]

9

"RANE MAT'TAI PAKLEANKO" (Ranes are killing the Portuguese)

This essay was written originally for inclusion in a Goa University publication to commemorate Silver Jubilee of Goa's Liberation. The paper was deemed improper and was unceremoniously rejected as the official historians subservient to ruling political interests were only interested in paying floral tributes to Goa's freedom struggle, or whatever they chose to understand by that. Unfortunately, even the institution that is meant to set the tone for our intellectual life, including historical research, joined the chorus with 'Goa Wins Freedom'. This is the state of intellectual subservience and poverty twenty-five years after our liberation! And there are all the indications in our country that this tendency is on the rise.

The following exercise is what some modern scholars engaged in "subaltern studies" call historical 'deconstruction'. Our post-liberation historiography should not uncritically replace one elitist approach by another if political change in Goa is to serve truly democratic goals. We have an opportunity to put the "subaltern" or subordinate classes at the centre stage of our historical inquiry. Deconstruction in this context, is only a tool of analysis that seeks to attack and break down the existing elitist paradigms. It is not a nihilistic exercise, but a prolonged critical exercise to clear off the rubbish and prepare the ground for a sound alternative construction in the scheme of post-liberation historiography of Goa. What has been done here is to apply deconstruction analysis to one historical episode, namely the Rane myth in Goa's freedom struggle. Similar exercises will need to be extended to wider areas of Goa's history.

Truth is said to be stranger than fiction. The role attributed to the Ranes in Goa's freedom struggle is one illustration of this old dictum.

Folklore and, more recent political developments seem to have conspired to elevate the so-called 'Rajputs' of Satari to unquestioned honours as Goa's freedom fighters. Folklorising and political myth-making had its reasons and validity as means to sustain anti-colonial campaign. But twenty-five years after liberation we should be able to put aside political emotionalism and let historical criticism have its say.

How good is the Rane claim for Rajput origin? An anthropological study conducted by Dr. Germano de Silva Correia took the tradition of Rajput origin for granted, but the application of field techniques does not seem to have enabled him to confirm it decisively. He concluded saying: "Their ethnic origin remains an anthropoligical problem to be solved" (*Les Ranes de Satary*, 1928: 29). In the absence of further evidence, it remains to be proved that the Ranes of Satari differ essentially from the Marathas of the Deccan.

The origin of the Rajputs is a red herring that has been much dragged about in the historical writings on early-medieval and medieval India. One can observe an extreme polarity of opinions, which extends in range from attempts to trace the Rajputs to foreign immigrant stocks of the post-Gupta period, to contrived justifications for viewing the Rajputs as of pure *Kshatriya* origin. The question of the indigenous origin of the Rajputs assumed symbolic overtones in the heyday of nationalist historiography; and in the historical and purely literary writings of various genres, the military and chivalrous qualities of the Rajputs were repeatedly projected. All such writings tended to suggest that the Rajputs rose to prominence in the process of resisting foreign invasion and that they shouldered willingly the *Kshatriya* duty of fighting for the land as well as for its people and culture.

Even in detailed studies of Rajasthan, the origin of the Rajputs in the early medieval period is far from settled, and much less examined. There were widespread claims in the early medieval period to the traditional *Kshatriya* status. Such claims were attempts to get away from, rather than reveal, the original ancestry. It was a process in which new social groups sought various symbols for the legitimisation of their newly-gained power. The case of the Ranes of Satari can be taken to illustrate a similar process of mobility to Kshatriya status in this part of western India.

While elsewhere in the New Conquests the traditional village community set-up suffered some destruction under their Dessais, the village communities of Satari ceased to exist as a result of the recurring feuds among the Ranes themselves and their attempts to assert their own feudal control and relative independence. This is very important historical background to be taken into consideration while critically assessing the so-called contribution of the Ranes of Goa's freedom struggle. Freedom, as we now tend to understand it, seems to have been the last thing the Ranes aspired to.

In a taluka that is blessed with abundant natural resources, its own *ganvkars* inhabiting its original seventy or so villages, were reduced to misery and beggary. Even the traditional Dessais and Nadkarnis were marginalised by the Sardesai Ranes who established their *mokasas* all over the fertile and cultivable low-lying western region of the taluka and extended their administrative and fiscal control over the rest of the taluka. The armed force of the Ranes was assisted in this task by their brahmin Dubhashis. The Ranes also patronised hordes of Bhats who descended from across the Ghats into Satari to perform their religious role of preaching the oppressed local population into submission to their new overlords, smoothening thereby the mechanism of violence and reducing the administrative costs. The Bhats were generously rewarded with many *deussuns* and areca groves. The Bhats grew in numbers and wealth just as the native *ganvkars* decreased in numbers and increased in misery. All that was left to them were places of worship and beliefs about the nobility of the Ranes.

We do not have much documentary evidence that could throw light upon the efforts of the Satari ganvkars and their traditional leaders to resist the oppression of the Ranes until the time when the region came under the Portuguese jurisdiction. As in the case of most subaltern classes they were hardly in a position to produce records of their protest. But we do have, for instance, a long representation submitted by a dozen *ganvkars* of various villages of Satari to the Portuguese Governor of Goa, D. Manoel da Camara in April 1824. The document listed the grievance of the villagers against the Ranes and their 'tyrannical yoke' which had obliged many to seek refuge in the Portuguese territory and beyond the Ghats. They were pleading with the Portuguese Government to protect them by taking direct charge of the villages of Satari and their revenue administration. It is very probable that this representation was inspired and drafted by the Nadkarnis of Sanklli. While these Nadkarnis pretended concern for the plight of the village ganvkars, they were actually interested in regaining their own lost traditional control. With their proverbial skill to manipulate accounts and property records, in the 1830s the Nadkarnis of Sanklli nearly succeeded in settling old scores with the Ranes. Some details of this case could better help understand the complexity of interests in conflict and to realise that the Ranes did not represent the natives of Satari in their so-called freedom struggle.

The Nadkarnis represented traditional village interests and kept up their own freedom struggle against the Ranes. Obviously, they were no match to the Ranes in military skill and force, but they relentlessly pursued their struggle with traditional chicanery and cunning. The Nadkarnis and their agents had infiltrated into the Portuguese administrative ranks. Soon after the disturbances created by the Ranes which coincided with the political instability caused by the liberal-constitutional struggle in Goa (1822-1835), the Nadkarnis got round the Portuguese administration to frame a case against the Ranes for defrauding the Portuguese administration since 1746. In the process of fiscal inquiry entrusted by the Portuguese Government to a certain Atmaram Parab, the Nadkarnis, Dessais and *ganvkars* of Satari produced 'documented' information to prove that the Ranes had been paying revenue dues to the Sawants of Wadi in lieu of the *mokasas*. Hence, in keeping with the terms of submission to the Portuguese, the Ranes ought to have paid the same dues to the Portuguese exchequer. Obviously, the Nadkarnis would get back into the job of administering the revenue collection and of playing the power game that goes with it.

Luckily for the Ranes, their defence counsel managed to checkmate the judicial aspersions cast by the accusation of tax evasion by proving that Lakshman Kustam Sinai Nadkarni of Sanklli had cooked up the information supplied to Atmaram Parab and also forged documents in old Marathi using the seals of the Sawants. Another Nadkarni of Sanklli, Mallapa Sinai was also involved. They had also roped in the official State translator (*Língua do Estado*) Sakharam Narayan Vaga. His handwriting was identified in interpolations made on the 'Book of Peace treaties' (*Livro de Pazes*) in the Secretariat archives.

It is apparent from the above case that the Ranes had enemies from within. The traditional landed interests were not reconciled to being subjected to their power and ambitions. Any critical study of the recurring rebellions and disturbances caused by the Ranes will have to take into account the machinations and schemings of the Nadkarnis of Satari. What appears often as a straight Rane-Portuguese conflict will then be seen as a more complex situation in which the "subaltern" classes of Satari silently, or rather subtly, participated in the contest and sought to undermine the dominance of the Ranes.

It was not in the interest of the Portuguese to deprive the Ranes of their privileges in Satari because they had served as a useful *contra* force to check the adventurism of the Marathas. Alarmed by Shivaji's attempts to extend his sway in the Konkan, the Portuguese continued to support the turbulent Dessais of Kudal, Pedne, Bicholim and Sanklli in resisting the territorial ambitions of the Maratha chieftains of the Deccan. Contrary to the myth propagated by most traditional historians that all Marathas (if not all Hindus) had enthusiastically rallied round Shivaji's banner and his *Hindavi Swarajya*, an eminent and critical Maratha historian, Prof. A. R. Kulkarni tells us that "the people of the Konkan never associated themselves with the Maratha movement launched by Shivaji...Shivaji did succeed in capturing some parts of the Konkan, but the core of Konkan which was under the Dessais and the Portuguese never came under the Maratha control".

Unfortunately, since liberation Goans are being taught their history by teachers from outside Goa who have an insufficient grasp of the local ethos and cultural background. We read in the '*Goa Gazetteer*' that "the aim of these wars (revolts of Ranes) was to regain the lost territory and freedom. The Ranes were supported by the common people who were eager to sweep out the intolerant, obnoxious rule of the Portuguese". No critical historian could state that the native population that was reduced to serfdom by the Ranes had the option to choose whether to join them (the Ranes) or not in their resistance to those who attempted to check their banditry.

The Ranes backed any neighbouring ruler (including the Portuguese) when it suited them, and they backed out from repeatedly renewed "oaths of fealty" to the Portuguese whenever it did not suit their interests. That the "common people" of Satari should have "supported the Ranes" can best be understood from the analysis of a modern and critical Maratha historian, Prof P. V. Ranade: "Robbing the rich for the benefit of the poor is an instinct of all primitive rebellions. Shivaji's campaigns of *mulukhgiri* into Mughal territories were campaigns of plunder against rich emporiums and must have thrilled the hearts of the 'naked rascals'. Shivaji was shrewd enough to exploit this primitive instinct. Thus he and his successors (applicable to Ranes) could enlist the Maratha bargirs and shiledars in the *mulukhgiri* campaigns on the basis of an appeal to their predatory instinct and religious ethos".

There are several instances of the Ranes serving the Portuguese as mercenaries in Goa as well as far away from it in Ceylon during the 17th century. In the 18th century we find them serving the Portuguese as feudatories that were not always reliable. But that was nothing unusual in the feudal set-up. The doyen of Indian historians, Prof. D. D.

Kosambi, a Goan by origin, states in his classic *An Introduction to Indian History* that, with their depredations till the end of the last century, the Ranes were no better than "robbers claiming feudal titles". The evidence and analysis he provides tend to confirm such an assessment. The Ranes only sought to preserve and enlarge their feudal privileges. Once under the Portuguese suzerainty since 1746, the clash between Portuguese colonial interests and their own feudal interests became inevitable. This is exactly what happened. The only option open to the Ranes was to shake off Portuguese fiscal controls, or submit to their encroachment and eroding power at the expense of their own feudal claims.

Faced with the above alternatives the Ranes tried solutions of despair. They were ill-matched to face the superior organisational and military powers of the Portuguese. This was true despite the apparent inability of the Portuguese to quell the rebellions without compromises and grants of amnesty. The Rane Revolts coincided with a very disturbed political period in Goa. A time arrived when new and powerful economic interests which had entered Satari finally crushed their ambitions: over 26,000,arces of land were taken over on long leases by industrial interests for large-scale plantations. Some of these planters were British and American citizens. In the wake of the establishment of the railroad by the British in and around Goa, the timber wealth of Satari attracted exploiters. And increasing administrative co-operation and co-ordination between Goa and British India made it increasingly difficult for the Ranes to carry on their traditional game of hit-and-run.

The revolts of the Ranes were woven into a myth of freedom struggle and even provided themes for Konkani folk songs as a result of the growing political discontent among the native intelligentsia of the Old Conquests of Goa. The Pinto Revolt, the Peres da Silva affair, and the liberal-political struggle provide the background and clues which account for the transformation of Satari's feudal lords into legendary freedom fighters.

[Reprinted from *Goa Today*, Panjim, March 1987, pp. 28-33].

10

THE CHURCH AND GOAN LIBERATION

Nicodemus, a leading Jew, Pharisee and a politician who played it safe, once approached Jesus in the dark of night to seek his divine advice. He left puzzled with the dilemma of remaining an adult and being born again and from above (Gospel of St. John 3: 1-5). Elsewhere in the Gospels, one comes across the warning: "Anyone who does not welcome the Kingdom of God like a little child will never enter it" (Mt. 19: 14; Lk. 18: 16, Mk. 10 : 14). The *Bible* is also replete with metaphors of sheep and lambs. They are used to identify the faithful ones, the heirs to heaven.

Interpretations and misinterpretations of such scriptural texts have contributed to promote a Christian ethos in which passive submission to authority is identified with virtue and dissent with irreverence. This socio-religious aberration is not unique to Christianity, but in the context of its alliance with colonialism it became a serious hindrance to people's struggle for freedom. If Goa's freedom struggle was pioneered by men like Julião Menezes, Tristão Bragança de Cunha, Luis de Menezes Bragança and some others born Christians, it was their aversion to the Portuguese brand of Christianity that made them avowed patriots.

Most Goan Christians who were faithful to the Goan Church magisterium collaborated with the Portuguese civilizing mission that made of them a cultural tragicomedy. This mission was freshly re-emphasized by Dr. Oliveira Salazar through the Acto Colonial of the *Estado Novo*, and the predecessor of the last Portuguese Patriarch of Goa made a fine art of this civilizing mission of the Portuguese in their "overseas province" in India. His *Cartas aos Sacerdotes da Arquidiocese* (Letters to the Priests of the Archdiocese), numbering about sixty or so, constitute a masterpiece of a magisterial teaching of the church wedded to Portuguese nation.

The masses of Goan faithful were taught to believe that their salvation lay with the Portuguese and in disassociating themselves from the cultural-political relationship with the rest of India. More recently, every time that India was expected to make a move to liberate Goa, pilgrimages were arranged from Panjim to the tomb of St. Francis Xavier in Old Goa to pray to the Saint to deliver them from deliverance. It was rather broadminded of the Portuguese to trust so much in the Saint, who in his life-time wrote strongly against their zeal in Portuguese India and elsewhere in their empire to conjugate wrong verbs and with wrong people! It was his failure to change these attitudes and restrain such zeal that took him almost in desperation to distant fields of mission in the Far East.

In spite of Portugal's long history of anti-clericalism and unhappy relations with the Vatican, the New State (*Estado Novo*) of Salazar tried to uphold the ghost of the *Padroado*. The great statesman, described by some as a good Catholic but a bad man, saw no ambiguity of his actions till the end. His orders to adopt a scorched earth policy before abandoning the Rome of the East in 1961 marked the tail-end of a story that had begun four and half centuries ago. The Portuguese were saved from ending their civilising mission with an act of barbarity by Dr. Abel Colaço, a Goan Christian, who had understood his Christianity better than the foreign masters. It was the intervention of this high-ranking official that got Patriarch José Alvernaz to help an undeciding General to ignore the orders of Salazar.

It would be unfair to bypass a section of Goan Christians that made its contribution to Goa's freedom struggle and at the same time retained all its love for the traditional Goan Christianity minus its Portuguese mentors and lackeys — in priestly garb or otherwise. Because of this package deal available to Goan Christians, these stray sheep were forced, at various times, to change their domicile to the neighbouring Indian territory. Of course, that was also the only alternative for most Goans who could not be accommodated in the non-existent Portuguese industry and stagnating agriculture.

The Goan Christians who maintained a steady pressure campaign in favour of Goa's liberation from Bombay and elsewhere had no hang-ups like the Goan Christians inside Goa. They had the example of Cardinal Gracias of Bombay and many other prominent Goan clergymen who had come out openly in their condemnation of the Portuguese colonial rule in Goa and had demanded that it should end. However, the active participation of these Christians through physical means of violence or even of peaceful *satyagraha* was minimal, if not totally absent. And all this, in spite of the Goan Christian community being more affected by the economic blockade imposed by Indian authorities and the tax imposed by the Portuguese authorities upon their money remittances to relatives in Goa.

My one conclusion is that if this section of Goan Christians were behaving as naughty children in the eyes of the Portuguese patronized church, they were behaving as children all the same. They retained all the timidity and unwillingness to risk by confronting the State authorities that was characteristic of Goan Christians, and perhaps of all Christians suffering from a minority complex. They kept up the old game of wait-and-see till it was safe to take sides and have a share in the gains. One stalwart of the Bombay-based Goan Christians had even coined a slogan with his penchant for rhetoric: "Rome-rule is home-rule"! He was knighted, for sure, with a papal award, but it did not enhance the importance of the contribution of the Bombay-based Goan Christians to Goa's liberation struggle.

To complete my picture of Goan Christianity and its stand *vis-a-vis* Goa's struggle for freedom it would be too facile a generalisation to lay at the feet of Christians alone the responsibility for the obvious absence of a mass liberation movement in Goa. To quote Julião Menezes in his *Goa's Freedom Struggle* (1947): "There is clear evidence to show that the Hindu Sabhites among the Goan Hindus have joined hands with Catholic Action agents" and "a large number of Saraswat Brahmins are collaborating with Catholic Actionists and the Portuguese Government ... Some of these men are even misusing the name and authority of the National Congress (Goa)".

In such a murky situation of the pre-liberation days it is difficult to assign to any single community the glory of untarnished championship of Goa's freedom struggle. V.N. Lawande (the *Loundo* that had stuck terror in the ranks of the Portuguese rulers and their native collaborators) admitted, during the proceedings of an Oral History Seminar organized by the Xavier Centre of Historical Research a couple of years ago, that he had experienced much goodwill among many village Christians in the course of his terrorist campaign. Once he was nearly trapped by the Portuguese police inside a village in Tiswadi taluka, but the police failed to detect their most-wanted man who crossed their roadblock in a car donning a priest's soutane and saying beads. This life-saving ruse was made possible by a sympathetic Christian family.

Lawande also admitted that the Christians who were sympathetic to the freedom-struggle would have been more emotionally involved if they could keep in touch with developments through papers and leaflets that were more easily accessible to the Marathi-reading Goan Hindus.

The liberation of Goa was impossible without direct intervention of the Indian armed forces. However, if the Operation Vijay was effected at the close of 1961, its urgency was dictated more by the prospects of the ruling party in the national elections that were scheduled for February 1962, and even more by India's diplomatic stakes in the non-aligned movement. At the Belgrade Conference in September 1961 India's leadership seemed questioned by the African block struggling against the Portuguese colonialism. Though India had been the initiator of the anti-colonial revolution, she appeared to have lost her militancy. The African block claimed that a strong action by Nehru in Goa would enhance and even make easier the African revolution, a claim that would be confirmed by General Spinola in his *Portugal e o Futuro* in 1974. There was also China working hard to undercut Nehru's leadership of the Afro-Asian states. It was to counter these trends and to refurbish his image that Nehru was compelled to sponsor a seminar on Portuguese Colonialism in Delhi beginning October 20. Operation Vijay became an unavoidable next step.

What was happening in the meantime on the Church front? While the press at the local, national and international levels was agog with news of an imminent intervention by India to end Portuguese colonialism which it defined in the world forum as "a permanent aggression on Indian nationalism", the official bulletin of Goa Archdiocese carried in its December 1961 issue a bold-face announcement that Rome had appointed D. José Pedro da Silva as the new Auxiliary Bishop for Goa and with the right for succession as Patriarch. This Azores-born country-cousin of the Patriarch Alvernaz was at this time based in Lisbon and in charge of the headquarters of the politically suspect Portuguese *Catholic Action Movement.* It looks as if no qualified and experienced Goan candidate was available for the post, and the approval of such a nomination by the Vatican at such a juncture of Goa's history seemed out of tune with the concerns that Vatican had just voiced so very forcefully around that time in Pope John XXIII's *Mater et Magistra.* Was it just a coincidence that soon after Portugal lost its control over Goa, the former Patriarch of Goa (1942-53), whom we have already mentioned as an ardent Portuguese patriot, should be made a Cardinal and given a job in the Vatican? Was it another instance of "be cunning as a serpent" - diplomacy of the Vatican? Was not the title of the Patriarch given to the Archdiocese of Goa as a sop to stop the whinning of the Padroado boys at a time when the Vatican decided to create an independent Indian Church hierarchy in 1886? And had not Rome sent a Golden Rose to Goa Archdiocese to soothe the Portuguese feelings in the wake of the Vatican decision to give independent India its first Cardinal? If the liberation of Goa did not cause any violent upheaval in the administration of the Church in Goa the Vatican diplomacy deserves the least credit for it. Even to see some good reason to retain the patriarchate in Goa (or rather to confer it upon a native Archbishop of Goa) it took the Vatican more time than the new Portuguese leftist rulers to renounce the relics of their *Padroado* rights!

Following Goa's liberation, the Portuguese Patriarch maintained, very wisely, a low profile. Fortunately, for him and for the Church in Goa, the inauguration of the second Vatican Council in Rome provided the best excuse to end his uneasy stay in Goa before the end of 1962. Msgr. Francisco Xavier da Piedade Rebello then emerged as the head of the Church in Goa and he was consecrated Bishop and Administrator Apostolic of Goa in 1963. He had silently served more than one Patriarch as Secretary, as Chancellor, and as Vicar General. Only the liberation made a recognition of his services possible. In the earlier political set-up he may have been found fit at best to rule over some diocese in Portuguese Africa.

The political developments of the post-Liberation period have been complex and do not lend themselves to simple explanations. A large section of the population and its ideological leadership were joyous at integration with India. The Portuguese-educated landed gentry preferred to nurse their disappointment within their closed gossip-circles or occasionally voiced it in the columns of *O Heraldo* which they patronized less with subscription and more by reading borrowed issues. The dreams of some about a Goan republic became irrelevant overnight.

The democratic process in Goa began where it should have begun, namely at the village level. Panchayati Raj was brought into existence within less than a year after liberation. The elections held in October 1962 changed the entire character of the political process in Goa. No elections of the Portuguese-type had any parallel with the universal suffrage that brought the propertyless and uneducated masses into consideration for the first time. The elections for the first State Assembly the following year further strengthened the process. The classes that had been most neglected by the Portuguese, and consequently by the more advanced classes of the people of Goa, suddenly shot to power. Hindu Brahmins and Christian *bhatkars* entered a period of expiation for past sins.

The Maharashtrawadi Gomantak Party (MGP) and its *Bahujan Samaj* ideology was an expression of populism that sought to whip up communal feelings. The Marathi language was used for this along with merger issue. The penetration of the rural electorate was also done most effectively with promises of land reforms that would give land to the tiller. As most tenants were non-Christian and non-Brahmin, the MGP forced a response of these sections in self-defence. While the Hindu elite vote got divided between the Congress and United Goans Party (UGP), most Christians regardless of class or caste rallied round the UGP in spite of the fact that mass conversions effected four and half centuries ago had not made them equal through baptism, either socially or economically.

The victory of the MGP with an absolute majority in the first elections and its continued rule over Goa for more than a decade may be considered as the best thing that could happen to the majority of the Goans who had for too long been denied their rightful place. The personality and innate populist style of operating of the late D. B. Bandodkar gave the downtrodden, for the first time in their lives a sense of self-importance, which the traditional élite classes interpreted as vulgar insolence. Even if the social justice under the new dispensation only meant a shifting of injustice from one area of the population to another, the new rule marked a sharp break from the past quasi-feudal ethos that prevailed in Goa. Any other party in power at this critical time in Goa's history might have only replaced the old foreign colonial rule with a milder (?) native version of it.

Even if, in the wake of liberation, the Christians had to experience the other end of the stick, they woke up to realize that without learning the ropes of realpolitik they had no chances of survival in the new game of democratic politics. The Christians did play their role responsibly and effectively in fighting against merger through the Opinion Poll of 1967. This marked the end of one major phase in Goa's political process and initiated politics of new alliances that brought Goa into the mainstream of national politics from the late 70's. In the new scenario, religion and caste continue to provide pre-given organizational and mobilisational platforms, but political alliances follow more the class interests of the propertied sections with populist leadership. Much of the old élite has made a political come-back and the Christians had never done it better than as at now. They even provided the first Goan minister ever in the Union Government of Mr. Gandhi.

The democratic revolution experienced in Goa by the less mortal Christian laymen was not without its effects upon the hierarchical set-up. Everything had been calm and sheepish during the times of Church-State alliance. In the wake of the liberation the new winds kicked up quite some dust, and at times threatened to blow into storms. However, the forces of inertia have proved to be more deep-seated within the ramparts of the *Paço Patriarcal* than in the Church outside it. It had to be shaken out of its sluggishness through challenges that came from the Government quarters and also from its own faithful subjects, both men and women. Curiously, from the ladies first. I am referring to Nossa Senhora de Piedade Institute case. Even in God's name the Church authorities could not anymore be a law unto themselves. Neither the top leadership nor the general run of the clergy seemed to be prepared to meet the new challenges with self-confidence and with equanimity.

It is important, however, to note that the Church in Goa has been facing, in the post-Liberation period, not just the forces released by the political liberation, but also the upheaval caused by the second Vatican Council. Many problems of the Church in Goa were to some extent also the problems of the Church worldwide, and to that extent one can sympathize with the Church trying to grapple with a two-fold revolution. Vatican II was a force that seized the mind of the Roman Catholic Church and carried it across centuries, from the 13th to the 20th. The Church in many ways had been fixed immovably, held in a kind of wrought-iron vision of its own immutability. Vatican II opened the institution to change. The vocabularies and trappings of eternity dropped away, and the Church recovered its vision of a pilgrim Church that should be open to risk and to constant renewal. To my mind, the political liberation was a timely blessing for the Christianity in Goa. It provided the best possible set-up to evolve a spirituality that was integrated with struggles of existence, to grow as citizens of heaven but fully involved in the building of the city on earth. It was an enviable opportunity to "be born again", to start life afresh with the freedom of the children of God and of the mother country. It was a challenge to cast off the old mould into which the Christianity had been frozen, and to stop living as crippled children. It was a challenge to rise and walk. The Gospel challenge thrown to Nicodemus retained all its validity for the Church of Goa in the post-Liberation and post-Vatican II era.

The Church of Goa is definitely more alive today, and it is alive precisely because of all the unpleasant conflicts that it has to face. The Church had entered the field of education in a big way. At least twenty new religious congregations of women and men have entered Goa since 1961 and have initiated new work that care for the aged, destitute and the handicapped. The Church has made its presence felt in areas where gross violation of social justice was taking place. The Church has taken steps for financial reforms since the 70s and more recently it has tried to regulate a just salary for its lay workers. The Church today is also more open to lay participation. These are some of the more outstanding gains and signs of new life.

However, the balance sheet has also been marred by an overbearing attitude of the hierarchy on different occasions, when a more pastoral approach and kindness could have produced better results. The openness to laity has not resulted in greater accountability of the clerical functioning to the laity, neither has the lay participation taken into confidence lay persons of less dominant social classes. The involvement in education remains very slipshod. It is collaborating with the Government system to mass-produce educated unemployment and to increase the number of drop-outs that has reached an alarming 87 per cent at the SSC level. The Church has also failed to train better and trust more its younger clergy. The leadership required in the post-Liberation era cannot be expected from the young priests if the old system of promotions and incentives (or lack of them) is continued. But the winds of change are definitely at work, though one wishes the mills of Gods did't have to grind so slowly!

[Revised version of "Goan Catholicism and Liberation" in *Goa Today* (Panjim), December 1986, pp. 47-51].

PUBLICATIONS OF THE AUTHOR (1972-1993)

"A Study of the Indo-Portuguese Coinage and the Working of the Goa Mint", *Indian Numismatic Chronicle* 10 (1972):67-72.

"A work of painstaking research" (Book Review), *Goa Today*, December, 1973: 32.

"*Xenddi*-tax: A Phase in the History of Luso-Hindu Relations in Goa, 1704-1841", *Studies in the Foreign Relations of India* (H.K. Sherwani Felicitation Volume), ed.P.M.Joshi and M.A. Nayeem, Hyderabad, 1975:462-71.

"Goa-based Portuguese Seaborne Trade in the Early Seventeenth Century", *The Indian Economic and Social History Review*, XII, 1975: 27-35.

"Glimpses of Hindu Dominance of Goan Economy in the 17th Century", *Indica*, XII, 1975:27-35.

"Matheus de Castro Mahale: An Unsung Hero", *Goa Today,* January 1975: 18,28.

"Portuguese Records for Indian History at Goa and Lisbon", *The Indian Archives,* XXV, 1976: 24-36.

"Goan Agrarian Economy in Crisis", *Itihas*, I, 1976: 55-70.

"Why no Menezes priest in Malar", *Goa Today*, November 1976: 13.

"Marine Insurance in Indo-Portuguese Trade History", *The Indian Economic and Social History Review,* XIV, 1977:24-36.

"A Tentative Check-list of Abbreviations in Portuguese Archival Records,"*Indica*, XIV, 1977: 117-24.

"The Language of Goans", *Goa Today*, March 1977:13-14.

"A pious Hindu commemorates in marble the activities of the Paulists in Kumbarjua", *Goa Today,* February, 1977: 14,22.

"Vatican II in India in the 17th Century: The genius of Robert de Nobili", *The Herald* (Calcutta), Sept. 30, 1977.

"Mariano Saldanha: A Centenary Tribute", *Indica,* XV, 1978: 135-39.

"Portuguese Source-Material in the Goa Archives for the Economic History of Konkan in the 16th and 17th Centuries", *Sources of the History of India,* I, ed. S.P. Sen, Calcutta, 1978: 426-41.

"Hindu entrepreneurship in Goan history", *Goa Today,* January, 1978: 15,18.

Medieval Goa: A Socio-Economic History, New Delhi, 1979: 315pp.

"Jesuits and Trade"(Open Forum), *The Times of India,* January 14, 1979: 8.

"Mhamai House Records: Indigenous Sources for Indo- Portuguese Historiography", *Proceedings of the Indian History Congress,* Bombay session, 1980: 435-45.

"C.R. Boxer, Portuguese India in the Mid Seventeenth Century" (Book Review), *The Indian Economic and Social History Review,* XVII, 1980: 422-23.

"Voiceless in Goan Historiography: A case for the Church records in Goa", *Indo-Portuguese History: Sources and Problems,* ed. J. Correia-Afonso, Bombay, 1981:114-31.

"B.S. Shastry, Studies in Indo-Portuguese History" (Book Review), *Indica,* XVIII, 1981: 141-42.

"Mhamai House Records: Indigenous Sources for Indo- Portuguese Historiography", *The Indian Archives,* XXXI, n.1, Jan.-June 1982: 25-45.

"M.N. Pearson, Coastal Western India" (Book Review), *The Indian Archives,* XXXI, 1982: 89-91.

"A Scholar's Discovery of Goa", *Alvaro de Loyola Furtado:A Tribute from his Fellow Citizens,* Margão, 1982: 52-54.

"J. Ferraro Vaz, Dinheiro Luso-Indiano" (Book Review), *The Book Review,* VII, 1983: 192-94.

"Heads Lose, Tails Win: Portuguese Currency", *Goa: Cultural Patterns,* ed. S.V. Doshi (Marg Publications),Bombay, 1983: 97-100.

"Foreign elements in the Rural Economy of Goa during sixteenth and seventeenth centuries", *Western Colonial Policy,* II, ed. N.R. Ray, Calcutta, 1983: 269-84.

"Capital Input in Goa's Freedom Struggle: The Bombay Connection", *Rojnishi,* I, n.2, ed. T.R. de Souza, (Poona University, Deptt. of History), 1983: 8-15.

"K.S. Mathew, Portuguese Trade with India in the Sixteenth Century" (Book Review), *Social Action,* XXXIV, Jan.-March 1984: 94-96.

Indo-Portuguese History: Old Issues, New Questions, ed. Teotonio R. de Souza (Select Proceedings of the 3rd international seminar on Indo-Portuguese History, Goa, 1983), New Delhi, 1985 (pp. 240).

"To the Nations and Nation: The Apostle of the Indies and the Apostle of Ceylon", *Renovação* (Goa archdiocesan bulletin), XV, n.4, Feb. 1985: 65-67. Also in *Ignis (Jesuit Indian Assistancy Journal of Ignatian studies),* 87-88, March- August 1985: 33-38.

"Spiritual Conquest of the East: A Critique of the Church Historiography of Portuguese Asia", *Indian Church History Review,* XIX, n.1, June 1985: 10-24.

"The Church won't carry the Cross", *Goa Today,* February,1986: 50-51.

"A conquista espiritual do Oriente: Nota crítica sobre a historiografia da Igreja na Asia Portuguesa", *Para uma história da Igreja na America Latina*, ed. Jose Beozzo, Petropolis, 1986: 123-135.

"Jesuit Records in Portuguese on Shivaji's South Indian Campaign and its impact on the people", *Indica*, XXIII,March- Sept. 1986: 89-100.

"Goan Catholicism and the Liberation", *Goa Today*, December 1986: 47-51.

"Some historical notes on Moira", *Moira: A peep into its past* (Commemorative of 350 years of the village church), 1986: 1-12.

The Ranes of Sanquelim: Feudal Lords Unmasked", Goa Today, March 1987: 28-33.

"The Written Word Endangered", *Goa Today*, April 1987:33-35.

"Freedom for Service: Individually guided retreats", *Ignis*, vol.16, n.101, 1987: 31-38.

"New Source Material for the Socio-Economic History of the Hindus of Goa", *Goan Society Through the Ages*, ed. B.S. Shastry, New Delhi, 1987: 186-92.

"XXXII ICANAS" (A Report on the 32nd International Congress of the Asian and North African Studies), *Indica*, Vol.24, n.1 (March 1987): 62-63.

"Young Jesuits and Intellectual Standards", *Ignis*, XVI, 1987, n.6: 277-281.

"The Oratorians of Goa (1682-1836)", *Joseph Vaz: Herald of Christ*, Vol. I, n.3, 1987: 7-9; n.4, 1987: 4-6.

"The Afro-Asian Church in the Portuguese *Estado da India*", *Indian Church History* Review, XXI, n.2 (Dec.1987): 93- 114; *African Church Historiography: An Ecumenical Perspective*, ed. Ogbu U. Kalu, Bern, 1988: 56-76.

"The Portuguese in Asia and their Church Patronage", *Western Colonialism in Asia and Christianity*, ed. M.D. David, Bombay, 1988: 11-29.

"Peter under Peter", *Goa Today* (Jan. 1988): 37-38.

"Defining Goan Culture", *Goa Today* (Jan.'88): 43-46.

"Oratorians of Goa (1682-1835)", *Goa: Cultural Trends*, ed. P.P. Shirodkar, Panaji, 1988:141-50.

"Re-Writing the History of the Society of Jesus in India: Questions of facts and relevance", *Indian Missiological Review*, Vol.9, n.4 (October, 1987): 269-277; *Jesuit Presence in Indian History*, ed. Anand Amaladass, S.J., Satya Nilayam, Madras, 1988: 14-23.

"Manohar Malgonkar, Inside Goa" (Book Review), *The Indian Historical Review*, Vol.XI, nn.1-2 (July 1984-Jan.1985):245-47.

"The French-Mhamai connection", *The Herald*, Panjim, March 20, 1988: 3.

"The Emerging Church of the Poor", *Goa Today,* April 1988: 12-16.

"Seeds of Disharmony", *The Herald,* Panjim, April 27, 1988: 2; *Renovação* (Pastoral Bulletin of the Archdiocese of Goa), XVIII, June 1, 1988, n.11: 198-9.

"Looking from Goa", *International Goan Convention '88,* Toronto, 1988 : 52-53.

"History of Mozambique: An Introduction to Bibliography", *Purabhilekh-Puratatva* (Journal of the Directorate of Archives, Goa) Vol. VI, No.1, Jan.-June 1988: 63-77.

"K. M. Mathew, *History of the Portuguese Navigation in India, 1497-1600,* Africa Newsletter (ASSI), IV, n. 2:73.

Essays in Goan History, ed. Teotonio R. de Souza, New Delhi, 1989 (pp. 219).

"Church and Political Transition in Goa, 1961-1988", *Tripod* (Published by the Holy Spirit Study Centre, Hong Kong), n.2, 1989: 40-55.

"Fr. José Vaz and Fr. Agnelo de Sousa: The Struggle for Sainthood", *Goa Today,* Panjim, June 1989: 10-14.

"Joseph Thekkedath, History of Christianity in India, II, and A. M. Mundadan, History of Christianity in India, I, Theological Publications in India, Bangalore, 1982-1984" (Book Review), *The Indian Historical Review,* XIII, n. 1-2 (July 1986 & Jan. 1987): 283-5.

"Embassies and Surrogates", *Indica,* Vol. 26, nos. 1-2 (March-September 1989): 39-55.

"M. N. Pearson, The New Cambridge History of India, I.1: The Portuguese in India, Cambridge, 1987; and R. Ptak (ed.), *Portuguese Asia: Aspects in History and Economic History,* Stuttgart, 1987" (Book Review), *Indica,* Vol. 26, nos. 1-2 (March-Sept. 1989): 155-159.

Goa Through the Ages, II : An Economic History, ed. Teotonio R. de Souza (Goa University Publications Series, No.6), Concept Publ. Company, New Delhi, 1990 (pp.316).

"Goa-Mahe Trade Links: Late 18th-Early 19th Centuries", *Studies in Maritime History,* ed. K. S. Mathew, Pondicherry University, 1990, pp. 165-174

"Tradition of St. Thomas in India: Some Opinions", *CCBI News,* Panjim, Vol. I, nos. 1-3: 30-32, nos. 3-4: 63-68.

"Mariano Saldanha","P.S.S. Pissurlencar", "Rogerio de Faria", "José Nicolau de Fonseca", "D. Matheus de Castro", "José Gerson da Cunha", *Goa's Hall of Fame,* ed. Bailon de Sá (for the International Goan Youth Convention, Panjim, 17-27 Dec. 1990), pp.30-41, 51-2.

"Xavier Centre of Historical Research", *Handbook of Libraries, Archives and Information Centres in India,* Vol. 9, Part 2, ed. B.M. Gupta, Delhi, Adutya Prakashan, 1991, pp. 239-42.

"India and South Africa", *Herald*, Panjim, 4-5 March, 1991.

"Goan Culture and Identity: Historically Speaking", *Boletim do Instituto Menezes Braganza,* n. 162, 1991: 57-61.

"Men of Ignatius: The Jesuits in India", *Herald*, Panjim, 30th July, 1991.

"Some Outstanding Members of the Society of Jesus", *Herald*, Panjim, 31st July, 1991.

"Sanjay Subrahmanyam, Improvising Empire: Portuguese Trade and Settlement in the Bay of Bengal, 1500-1700, OUP, New Delhi, 1990" (Book Review), *Studies in History*, New Delhi, 7, 1, n.s. (1991): 173-176.

"A Question of Identity", *Goa Today*, August 1991: 24-25.

"Basic Christian Communities: From Roman Catholicism back to Early Church Catholicism", *Theology Annual*, Hong Kong, Vol. 12 (1990-1991), pp. 181-201.

"Local Churches: Some Historical-Theological Reflections in the Asian Context", *Theology Annual*, Hong Kong, Vol. 12, pp. 202-215.

Jesuits in India: In Historical Perspective, ed. Teotonio R. de Souza and Charles J. Borges, Macau, Instituto Cultural de Macau, 1992, pp. 413.

"Why Cuncolim Martyrs? An historical re-assessment", *Jesuits in India: In Historical Perspective,* ed. Teotonio R. de Souza & Charles J. Borges, Macau, 1992, pp. 37-47.

"Historical Background to Discoveries", *Social Action* (Special Issue on "Christopher Columbus: Five Centuries of Colonialism"), Jan.-March 1992, pp. 16-24.

"Church Card or People's Card in Goan Politics" *Boletim do Instituto Menezes Bragança*, No. 166 (1992), pp. 41-54.

"500 Years After: From the New World to the New World Order", *Boletim do Instituto Menezes Bragança*, No. 167 (1993), pp. 135-141.

"Christianization and cultural conflict in Goa: 16th - 19th centuries", *Congresso Internacional de História: Missionação Portuguesa e Encontro de Culturas,* Braga, 1993, Actas, IV — *Missionação: Problemática Geral e Sociedade Contemporânea*, pp. 383-93.

"Rogerio de Faria: An Indo-Portuguese Trader with China Links", *As Relações entre a India Portuguesa, a Asia do Sueste e o Extremo Oriente, Actas do VI Seminário Internacional de História Indo-Portuguesa,* ed. Artur T. de Matos e L.F. e Reis Thomaz, Macau, 1993, pp. 309-319.

"Some Guises of `Christ' in Asia", *Concilium*, April 1993.

"Gonçalo Martins: Jesuit Procurator, Businessman and Diplomat in the Estado da India", *Mare Liberum,* Lisboa, No. 5, Julho 1993, pp. 119-128.

INDEX